Voices *of*
Shoeburyness

Voices *of* Shoeburyness

Judith Williams

The History Press

First published 2010

The History Press
The Mill, Brimscombe Port
Stroud, Gloucestershire, GL5 2QG
www.thehistorypress.co.uk

British Library Cataloguing in Publication Data.
A catalogue record for this book is available from the British Library.

ISBN 978 0 7524 5223 4

Typesetting and origination by The History Press
Printed in India by Aegean Offset Printers, New Delhi

Contents

Acknowledgements

This book could not have been written without the help and co-operation of the interviewees who cheerfully and willingly gave up their time to assist me. Many have provided superb photographs from their own albums and leads to further contacts. Their generosity and the welcome I received into their homes made the research for this book an absolute delight.

I would particularly like to mention Bob Dack, Joyce Taylor, John Askew and Caroline Gibb – credit for the fantastic range of personalities that feature in the following pages goes to them. I would also like to thank Liz Alexander, Keith Barham, Gillian Blackall, Victoria Currell, Laurie Gaymer, Peter Owen, Margaret Rooke, John Taylor and Jim Worsdale for their help with providing photographs, information or contacts. Thanks also to Christine Selby for proofreading and to Tony Hill, whose knowledge and expertise were much-valued contributions.

My very sincere thanks to the 'stars' of the book: Peter Allen, Thomas Ambridge, Maureen Andrews (*née* Rawlings), John Askew, Ivy Atkins (*née* Davis), Roger Bacon, Keith Bailey, Joy Bateman (*née* Gilbey), Doreen Biles (*née* Scott), Peter Brewer, Angela Bowhill (*née* Brewer), Ann Burtle (*née* King), Gloria Burwell (*née* Everett), Margaret Chaplin (*née* Bates), Maureen Clark (*née* Keys), Ray Church, Alan Cundy, Robert Dack, Victor Davies, Les Dowie, June Edwards, Ken English, Dave Evans, Henry Evans, Terry Fane, Caroline Gibb, Gus Gundy, Margaret Hammond (*née* Newman), Arthur Haslehurst, Betty Harp (*née* Bates), Trevor Harp, Betty Harrington (*née* King), Joyce Henn (*née* Rawlings), Ron Henn, Tony Hill, Julia Kalogerides (*née* Everett), Brian Kane, Iris Lazell (*née* Wharton), Mary Major (*née* Prime), Robin Mann, Tom Mayhew, David Odell, Vivienne Odell (*née* Edwards), Derek Palmer, Vivien Pask (*née* Cox), Doreen Penlington (*née* Gilbey), John Perrin, John Prime, Michael Robinson, Gillian Saggers (*née* Emberson), Paul Scotchford, Dennis Smith, Joyce Taylor (*née* Robinson), Margaret Thorogood (*née* Clarke), Norma Tyler (*née* Cox), George Ventris, Pat Ventris (*née* Ling), John Wenning and Eileen Whalley (*née* Scott).

Introduction

The average age of my interviewees was seventy-six and most of the stories recounted here date from 1935–1955, with a few from the 1920s and 1960s. I have endeavoured to reproduce the stories exactly as they were told to me, although, due to lack of space, I have not been able to include all the memories in full. I apologise for any errors; this is no fault of the interviewees. Please remember that nobody is claiming 100 per cent accuracy in these stories; they are personal memories, from a personal point of view.

Individually, these stories are interesting; taken together they paint a vivid and fascinating picture of a Shoeburyness that will never been seen again. The overall consensus shines through: Shoebury was a wonderful place in which to grow up.

I hope you enjoy reading the memories as much as I have enjoyed recording them.

ONE

Early Memories

A BUSY WOMAN

Because my Dad was in the Army, me and my twin sister, Lily, were born in the Families Military Hospital on Campfield Road, which is now the Garrison Arms pub. I was there again when I was about three years old and had pneumonia, nearly ending up in the mortuary, which was down in the cellar.

There were nine of us children, so my mother had her work cut out when we were ill. She had six or seven of us with the measles all at once one time and had to call our doctor, Dr Paddy Ryan. He wasn't very pleased at being called out and said, 'I hope you know I'm a very busy man, Mrs Dack.' Mother replied, 'Well, you'll see I'm a very busy woman, Dr Ryan.'

We were alright because Dad was in the Army, but without a National Health Service, other people had to pay for a doctor. The unofficial midwife lived in Smith Street; we knew her as Molly. She used to ride round the town on her bike with a basket on the front and was always dressed in black. She brought a lot of Shoebury people into the world.

Bob Dack

POLICE IN THE FRONT ROOM

When I was four, we lived in a bungalow in Thorpedene Gardens backing onto Richmond Avenue School. Our front room was the local police station, before the station was built in Elm Road. Inspector Christie, who lodged with us, was in charge and also I remember Sergeant Cheatle.

On Saturdays we used to go to the pictures at the cinema known as the Bug 'utch. We saw two films and paid 1*d* downstairs and 2*d* up. We also used to go down the road next to the cinema and stand on the bridge watching the trains, ending up with black faces from the soot on the bars.

We used to play in the fields between Pentland Avenue and Thorpe Bay station and among the many malm banks. We also played in the brickfields, though we were always scared of being caught!

At the end of what is now Maplin Way there was Mason's boathouse, which burned down. My Uncle Jack was in charge of the car park near the beach huts and the lovely round Uncle Tom's Cabin, and I often went swimming with my dad at Shoebury beach.

Betty Harrington (née King)

BATH NIGHT

Mother did the washing in our tin bath on a stool in the kitchen. A similar bath was used every Friday night for our baths. My brother and I would sit on the kitchen table with towels wrapped around us listening to the gramophone and then Father would come in with a big, thick biscuit for us.

Doreen Biles (née Scott)

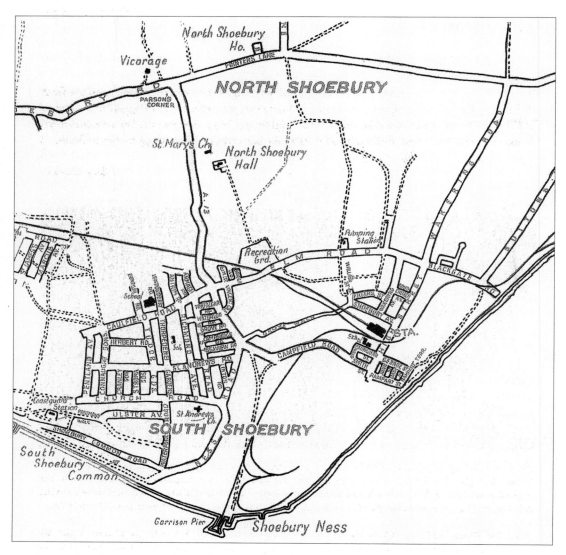

A map of Shoeburyness, around 1940, showing the limited extent of the town at that time. (John Prime)

BALLET AND TAP DANCING

Miss Ventris lived in St Andrew's Road, next door to Dr Ryan. She ran a girls' club once a week at St Andrew's church hall and Kathleen Grist, Southend's first Carnival Queen, came to teach us dancing – ballet and tap dancing. We took part in a show at the Palace Theatre; I did ballet and was 'Spring'.

In our Christmas stockings we had apples and oranges, a few nuts and perhaps some little tiny paints. There was usually a party for the children of railway workers and a British Legion party in their hall.

Eileen Whalley (née Scott)

UP A TREE WITH THE BOYS

When I was aged five we moved to a house in Shoebury High Street where we only used the front room for special occasions. Everyone seemed to know everyone else in the village. The fire engine was just up the road from us and I thought it was frightening. My mother worked as a cleaner down Blackgate Road and I used to climb up a tree with the boys while I was waiting for her to finish.

June Edwards

Above left: Jack Scott, aged eight, in his bandsman's uniform, 1928. Doreen Biles (*née* Scott) says, 'My dad and my brother, Jack, played in the Shoebury Silvertown Band. Dad wore a leopard skin and carried the big drum. Jack played the cornet from the age of eight and later became a soloist in the Royal Marines' band. In his youth, brother Jack also served as a lifeguard every Sunday morning at East Beach; he was a very good swimmer.' (Doreen Biles)

Above right: Vivien and Norma Cox with their mother in Pentland Avenue in the early 1950s. Vivien recalls: 'We used to play marbles out in the street in the gutter. We did skating, skipping and would swap stamps with our friends.' (Vivien Pask)

'BUNCHY THE BAKER'S DAUGHTER'

Until I married I lived behind and above Everett's the bakers shop: 12 High Street. I was known as 'Bunchy the baker's daughter', something to do with my curly hair, but it now sounds like somebody from an Enid Blyton story or a Happy Families game.

There were a few compensations to living in a bakers shop during the war as we probably had a little more rationed food than we would have had otherwise. I remember cutting the bread coupons from the rations books. One was allowed so much bread a week; a large loaf was 4 ½*d*, a small loaf 2 ¾*d*, and a roll one farthing.

We had an old carthorse called Kitty who pulled an enclosed cart along, in which the bread was delivered to both the village and the Cambridge end of Shoebury. I was allowed to sit high on the seat and help my father do his 'rounds' – no safety belt for me in those days! The round took us down the High Street to Wakering Road, Elm Road, Caulfield Road, Church Road, Campfield Road, through the garrison and back to the High Street, calling on dozens of other roads on the way home, in time for lunch. The trail that Kitty left was greatly prized by those who had allotments (and what a lot there were in Shoebury then!) and many a bucket and shovel followed us so that that contents could be 'put on the rhubarb'.

Kitty was then taken to a field in George Street, where she rested. When Kitty died, my father bought an electric van. We went very posh – away went the horse-drawn cart and the hand-pushed cart and we had a big box installed in our yard, where the van had to be 'charged' every night very much like my mobile phone is nowadays!

Gloria Burwell (née Everett)

HELPING WITH THE COAL ROUND

Before I was old enough to go to school, I used to go with my dad on his coal merchant's round, sitting up on the cart. From about 1926 he worked for Mr Offord who lived in Wakering Avenue and had a coal merchant's at the station. Dad's coal round took him from Shoebury to Wakering, then up to Barling and back. Dad also worked for the MoD, driving a locomotive in the ammunition dump on East Beach.

Dennis Smith

A GOOD LIFE FOR CHICKENS

We had rabbits and chickens at home, so after school we had to get green stuff for them or we'd go gleaning for chicken feed up Wakering Road. Dad knew the farmer and we were allowed to pick up ears of corn. Mr Galley used to come round with his horse and cart, bringing bran for the rabbits and poultry spice.

Our garden was quite big and we had about thirty rabbits and thirty chickens and they had a very good life. Apart from all the green stuff, Mum would put crusts of bread in the oven for the rabbits and when we had grown sprouts, she would hang up the root for the chickens to peck. Also, she'd boil potatoes with bran mash for the rabbits and give the chickens cod liver oil by holding them under one arm and opening their beak and pouring it in. On Saturdays, my sister and I had to clean out the rabbits.

Margaret Chaplin (née Bates)

DOGS AND RABBITS

Our dad worked on the railways for forty-nine years. One of his jobs was to clear out the carriages at the end of the day and he often found dogs in sacks under the seats, which people had left there. If you took them to the police they'd say, 'Get rid of it or keep it.' Nine times out of ten we kept it. One time, Mum went out to buy a bedspring and came home with a dog instead.

Dad kept two allotments and we had chickens and rabbits in the garden but we knew they weren't pets. Dad knew how to deal with them and sometimes when we came home from school there'd be one of our rabbits hanging up outside the back door. Apart from Dad's pet rabbit Woofles — he was different. Every night we'd set the table for the next day's breakfast and then Dad would insist on taking a crust of bread down to Woofles and we'd have to wait for him before we could go to bed. The corn man brought round the chicken food.

Doreen Penlington (née Gilbey)

Above left: Arthur Offord seen here on Nobby, who pulled the coal merchant's cart. Doreen Penlington remembers, 'A.J. Offord had a coal yard in Shoebury Avenue and a hut at the station but the family lived in Wakering Avenue. Arthur Jnr took over the business when his father retired.' (Doreen Penlington)

Above right: A party for local children held in the garrison theatre. (Pat Ventris)

MOVING TO SHOEBURY

Mum and Dad's first home at Shoebury was Bridge House Cottages. Dad had to go out to work as a cowman first thing and then come home for breakfast but on the first day, by the time he got home, Mum had put new curtains up and he didn't know what number he lived at.

I sometimes watched Mr Cook milk the cows at North Shoebury Hall Farm and once, when I was six years old, he turned the teat and squirted me with milk. I was furious and rushed home to tell my mum!

Iris Lazell (née Wharton)

DAD'S ALLOTMENT

When I came home from school at Monday lunchtimes, Mum would be washing and I'd turn the mangle for her. The water was collected in a galvanised bath and in the summer Dad used it to spray the broad beans for blackfly. He explained how it worked; you sprayed soapy water and it got into the blackflies' eyes – when they let go of the plants to wipe their eyes, they fell off.

Dad's allotment was at the top of Antrim Road; it was all fields and allotments from there up to the railway line. He grew potatoes, onions, carrots, cabbages and cauliflower. Salad stuff was grown in the garden – tomatoes and radishes and beautiful celery. Dad would tend the allotment for a couple of hours in the summer evenings after work and on Saturday and Sunday; Mum would tell me to 'volunteer' to help him.

It was nice and dry in our semi-sunk air raid shelter and we used to store vegetables in there – potatoes in their sacks, carrots in a bath of sand and onions hung up.

I spent quite a bit of time in Dad's shed when he was repairing things like the family's shoes. He had a last with three different size feet and a big tin containing leather, a leather knife, round heels held on with one screw, stick-on rubber soles (from Woolworths), small nails for fixing leather soles to shoes, and blakie heel and toe pieces. When Dad was repairing electrical appliances or plumbing, I was often sent round to the hardware shop in West Road with a pint bottle for paraffin. It could be quite exciting when Dad lit the blowlamp; if he pumped it before the paraffin was vaporising, there would be a jet of flame about 6ft long... but the shed survived!

Two or three nights a week Dad had to go to the electricity sub-station at Thorpe Bay and spend the night there in case it was bombed with incendiaries.

John Prime

ADVENTURE PLAYGROUND

Shoebury in the 1920s and '30s was a fascinating place. East Beach was a haven. There were two brickfields on East Beach, one of which was disused and made a wonderful adventure playground for the children. We had an area called the Red Pitch where we played cricket in the summer and football in the winter.

We also played football on Millbank's meadow. So did the men who worked on the brickfields up there. They worked until twelve o'clock, went home for their lunch, and then came back to play football.

Then, of course, we did a lot of cockling, musseling and winkling on the mud. We'd take them home and put half a cup of water to a saucepanful of cockles and boil them up on the stove.

Up at the Willow Patch there were two old sandpits full of water with ducks and swans on them. Of course, they cut down the willows and brambles when they built the Painters Estate there. From the Willow Patch, they would pump water to the brickfield washmills. A rail track ran from the mills to the Elm Road brickfields, with another line coming across to the High Street, crossing it near the Methodist Church.

Arthur Haslehurst

LOST A TOOTH AT FREEZERS

'Freezers', up by the footpath from the back of the cinema to the bridge at Elm Road, was a terrific place for children to play. There were ponds there and a stream that ran behind the cinema into the garrison, where we'd catch newts.

I got my tooth knocked out there in a catapult fight when I was about eight years old. I was defending the hill when a stone hit me right in the mouth and knocked it out – that was one of my best mates who did that! We often had fights up there, and made dens and lit fires. There was always a lot of people there.

'Bunkers' was the fields near the water tower. It was just fields and cows at that time, and malm pits down by Elm Road. The brickworks there were the main employers for the town, along with the railway and the AWRE.

We played football on the pitches near Shoebury Cottage.

Keith Bailey

ALL CLAPPING AND CHEERING

I was born in Shoebury High Street but later moved to Hinguar Street and then to Wakering Avenue. However, wherever home was, I spent half my life on East Beach, but with strict instructions not to go near the malm banks.

An early memory is of the boxer Larry Gains leaning out of the window of the Shoeburyness Hotel, and we were all clapping and cheering him.

I often played with the soldiers' children in the garrison. I was always in there; it was part of my youth. In all the years they were here there was never any trouble; a lot of Shoebury went when the Army went.

My mother told me not to play with Buster Ventris because he was too rough – so I married him!

Pat Ventris (née Ling)

Above left: Keith Bailey's Aunt Lil with her daughter in Grove Road. In the background is the garage run by Sid Bird who also ran a coach and taxi service. Grove Road and Cambridge Road were where Chelmer Avenue and Avon Road are now. (Keith Bailey)

Above right: The Methodist Sunday school behind the church, *c.* 1920. (Doreen Penlington)

FÊTES AND PARTIES

On May Day, Empire Day as it was then, the schoolchildren at Hinguar Street danced around the maypole. We all dressed in red, white and blue and I had a new red, white and blue dress for the occasion each year. Our school fêtes were held in the garrison on the cricket pitch but St George's Catholic Church held its fêtes on Gunners Park.

As we didn't have a back garden at the shop, I had my birthday party each year in the big garden at the back of Jeff's Café. Dad made all the cakes, etc., and I invited the whole of my class from school.

We used to play on East Beach and the brickfields running round and round the top of the malm banks, which I suppose was quite dangerous but we didn't think of that at the time. I spent most of my time down on the beach and used to take our cat out on the mud in my dolls' pram, dressed in dolls' clothes. After the floods in 1953, our beach hut was several hundred yards out on the mud, and most of the others destroyed.

Sometimes I went off on my bike with my friend. We'd go up to Wakering and cycle for miles. There were hardly any cars about, of course.

Once, there was a polio outbreak and Friars Street and Shoebury Avenue were cordoned off with no access. Sadly, a friend of mine died.

Julia Kalogerides (née Everett)

FEEDING THE FAMILY

Our family often went cockling, especially when our relations came down from London. We dug the cockles up with our fingers and could soon fill a couple of buckets. They were put in water overnight to clean themselves, then they'd be cooked in Mum's big electric copper.

When they were boiled, the shells would open and you could take them out and put them in jars with vinegar for the relatives to take home. It was then our job to bash up the cockle shells for grit for the chickens. Immediately after the war, we got blooming great big cockles because, of course, they'd been fattening up during all the years when people weren't allowed down on the beaches.

Mum would also bottle tomatoes and fruit in Kilner jars (we got our blackcurrants from a lady in Elm Road) and keep them in our big walk-in larder.

We also went potatoing when they were harrowing potatoes. The cut ones went in one sack, the little chittlings (which were about as big as my thumb) they did the chickens, and the good ones were for us.

Margaret Chaplin (née Bates)

CHRISTMAS

One Christmas during the war, Dad made me a lovely, wooden railway station with signals and lighting and a nice workbox for each of my sisters. Mum made all the clothes for their dolls and, in fact, made most of her own clothes. I got quite good at pinning up hems when she was making something for herself.

Christmas preparations began about a month before the 25th. Mum had gradually been saving dried fruit and nuts. The first thing to make would be the Christmas pudding. Mary and I would take the seeds out of the raisins and quite a few would be eaten whilst Mum was not looking! Then, once the pudding was in its basin, the argument with Mary and I was who was going to scrape out the mixing bowl. We also made flour and water paste to stick the paper chains together. All our parcels were tied up with string – no sellotape in those days – and the wrapping paper would be carefully folded up and stored for the next year.

Above left: A party in the Methodist church hall *c.* 1930. (Caroline Gibb)

Above right: Ivy Davis and Joy Leaney, back left, with other children in the Methodist Church, *c.* 1930. (Caroline Gibb)

Roger and Michael Bacon show off their decorated Easter eggs in the garden of 5 Hilly Marsh, Shoebury Garrison, *c.* 1952. (Roger Bacon)

Once or twice I was sent on my bike across on the ferry to Gravesend to collect a cockerel and some eggs from my uncle's chicken farm. I couldn't go on the train because it was illegal to transport chickens or eggs during the war and packages were searched.

John Prime

SUNDAYS AND CHRISTMASES

Our Sunday lunch was prepared on the Saturday night before. In the morning we went to Sunday school, then to church and then home for dinner. After dinner it was back to Sunday school, where Mum was a Sunday school teacher, followed by a walk over to Uncle Tom's. Then it was back to Granny's in Wakering Road for tea. Granny would start off by cutting brown bread and butter for Sunday night tea while I turned on the wireless for *Larry the Lamb*.

The loo was down the end of the garden, which was massive and full of fruit trees. Granny always said 'Don't eat the fruit!' and we would get a whack when we got back if we'd eaten any.

We'd go to church again at six o'clock on the Sunday evening. Then we had an apple or an orange and went to bed.

We had wonderful Christmases. On Christmas Day we had two cockerels, which Mum cooked. On Boxing Day we always had rabbit pie, which Dad cooked in a brown earthenware crock – he was fantastic.

Mum couldn't make a dozen mince pies, she'd make six dozen mince pies and six dozen sausage rolls. We'd have a cooked breakfast, then a full Christmas dinner, then port and nuts, then the Queen's speech, then tea and biscuits, then our Christmas tea with Congress tarts, then fruit and sweets (when we usually ended up with an orange peel fight), then at ten o'clock we'd have sandwiches – and we ate it all!

Our Christmas stocking really was just that – one of Mum's stockings. We got an orange, an apple, nuts, some pennies, perhaps some cheap perfume from Woolies or some crayons, and one present each.

Doreen Penlington (née Gilbey)

TWO

The Shoebury Landscape

SANDPIT COTTAGES, WAKERING ROAD – HAPPY FAMILY DAYS

For me, Shoeburyness in the 1920s represented the blissful two weeks' annual summer holiday at Granny's house, with its long garden of fruit trees, privy at the far end, all enfolded by old Farmer Layzell's cornfield.

Numbers 1 and 2 Sandpit Cottages had large, separate, brick-built outhouses and kitchens, known as the 'washers', but more properly the 'wash-house'. I well remember their long orchard gardens, vegetable plots, various sheds and chicken pens, and the wonderful view over the low boundary hedge of wide cornfield and surrounds, devoid of any nearby or overlooking buildings.

They were happy family days of summer with the day-long freedom of the beach and miles of sun-warmed mudflats to scamper over, just around the corner at the end of elm-shaded Blackgate Lane, a lovely cool avenue of trees leading to the beach.

John Perrin

NORTH SHOEBURY CORNER – HURRY TO GET THE WASHING IN

I was born at North Shoebury Corner, in a building that's now gone. The Post Office was next door but that was all; no other shops at all. When my sister Joyce spilt a cup of cocoa on herself, Mum took her across to the Post Office where they threw flour over her, so she wouldn't blister.

We used to go to Sunday school in the morning at St Mary's, church and Sunday school in the afternoon, and church again in the evening. I was very proud of my black patent shoes – they were our Sunday shoes.

My father used to mend all our shoes, cut all our hair and kept three allotments going, so we always had fresh vegetables, every day. The allotments were down a path from our house, quite a way. My mother's three washing lines were down there too. You came out of the gate and went down a path and down another path; everyone had washing lines down there. If it rained, you didn't half have to hurry to get the washing in!

Iris Lazell (née Wharton)

NORTH SHOEBURY CORNER – ROUTE MARCH TO THE TOILET

I once went to Sunday tea with a friend of mine who lived on North Shoebury Corner. After we had washed up and cleared away, I asked if I could use her toilet. 'Yes, just a minute and I'll come with you,' she said. 'Put your coat on.' So we put our coats on and she got a torch and then we went out the back door and on a route march right down in between the allotments in the pitch black and that's where the toilets were. I was used to a toilet indoors!

Betty Harp (née Bates)

Aerial photo of Shoeburyness, 1940. Vivien Pask says, 'We grew up in Pentland Avenue and there was nothing but cornfields between our house and Burgess Road. From our back bedroom window we could see the pier and the area around Bunters Avenue was cornfields up until about 1960.' (Keith Bailey)

June and Janet Perrin with their Great-Uncle John at the gate of 1 Sandpit Cottages, Wakering Road, c. 1935. (John Perrin)

North Shoebury Corner. Maureen Thorogood (*née* Clarke) remembers, 'The old Post Office at Parson's Corner had cockle shells and horseshoes pressed into the wall, the window ledges and in the cement on the ground around it.' (Footsteps Photos)

EARTHPIT COTTAGES – WASH-HOUSES AT THE BACK

I had a friend who lived in Earthpit Cottages, a terrace of wooden cottages just north of Elm Road. Each house had a garden out the front and four rooms inside. Behind the cottages was a brickyard with the wash-houses at the back of it. Round the back of the wash-houses were separate toilets for each cottage. The track beside the cottages led up to Millbank's Farm.

Joyce Henn (née Rawlings)

GOTHIC ROW – ONLY ONE TOILET

I lived in Gothic Row. There were families there with eight children or more. I think one family had twelve or fourteen, all in two rooms; one family lived in the two rooms downstairs and another family upstairs. There was only one toilet between seven houses and only one tap. There was only one tap in Baker's Yard as well.

Arthur Haslehurst

RAMPART STREET – ALL KEEN METHODISTS

When we lived in Rampart Street, Dad got up early to light the fire every Monday morning to boil a copper for the washing.

The front room was a tiny little square. The living room had a fireplace, a gas stove and a sink, but no tap – the only tap was in a brick-built scullery out the back. The stairs were very steep and at the top of the stairs was a large cupboard with a curtain over it – the bit over the passageway between the houses. There was one bedroom at the front and one at the back. The toilet, of course, was outside.

Our neighbour was a corporal in the garrison and on the other side of him lived Bill Ward, a bargeman for Eastwoods.

Then there was Nellie Kemp, who lived with her second husband, Wilf, who was on the railways – he would never have let the weeds grow on the tracks between Thorpe Bay and Shoeburyness like they do now! Mrs Kemp's unmarried brother was known as 'Old Shack', and they were all keen Methodists.

Further down Rampart Street were two dear old girls who kept a sweet shop, then the grocers run by 'Dribby' Parkins, who was in the Salvation Army.

Gunfire was our constant companion in those days, but I felt it was a friendly sound.

George Ventris

WAKERING AVENUE – 'STARVE GUT'

In 1940 we had to move out of the barracks – I suppose they needed the accommodation. We left behind a nice bathroom and went to Wakering Avenue, where we had one cold tap and a tin bath hanging in the cupboard. We only had one fire in a house of seven rooms and many-a-time I would wake up with dew on the top cover of my bed!

Wakering Avenue was built in two halves; the older part and the new houses, which were built about 1930. They called it 'starve gut' because in order to live there you had to go without other things. During the war we could hear the guns pounding but I don't remember being frightened.

Ron Henn

Rampart Street. Caroline Gibb says, 'People who lived in Rampart Street, John Street and George Street always left their front doors open. If the door wasn't open, it meant something was wrong and the neighbours would pop in to check up on you.'

Railway line buffers, photographed from the High Street. The poster advertises trips to Berwick-upon-Tweed. (Doreen Penlington)

SHOEBURY AVENUE – NO HEATING, NO HOT WATER

We had a three-bedroom terraced house in Shoebury Avenue with three rooms downstairs, no heating apart from coal fires and no hot water. The rear downstairs room had a coal-fired cast-iron range which was used in the winter for cooking and heating water in pans or kettles for us to bath in a galvanised bath that used to hang on the wall outside the scullery when not in use. When bathtime was over, the bath was carried out to the rear garden to be emptied. The scullery had one cold tap over a butler sink, which was all we had to wash in.

The rag-and-bone man came round with his horse and cart, and people could get a few bob for their old rags and scrap metal, etc. We were also visited by the ice cream man on a tricycle with an insulated box on the front in which the ice cream was kept cold, and the Corona van delivering soft drinks.

Brian Kane

SHOEBURY AVENUE – STEAM TRAINS AT 4 A.M.

When I lived in Shoebury Avenue we had the trains come along at the bottom of the garden. They would be getting up steam from about four o'clock in the morning. When you put your nappies out on the washing line you had to hope the wind didn't change because if it did you had to wash them all again. When people said it was a shame when the steam trains went, we didn't think so!

It was the tradition in Shoebury that when you got married and got on the train to go on honeymoon, the guard came along and locked you in the carriage and all the whistles started going. They used to sound all the whistles at New Year as well. And another thing you heard a lot of was fog horns.

Betty Harp (née Bates)

GROVE ROAD – NICE FAMILIES

There were a lot of nice families living in Grove Road and most of my friends were in the Grove Road gang. Like us in Ness Road, the houses had just a backyard with an outside toilet and a tin bath kept outside, hanging on the fence.

On the corner of Grove Road and West Road, two sisters had a sweet shop and owned a big orchard, which stretched alongside their house from where Chelmer Road is now to where Avon Road is. There was a lovely walnut tree at the end of the orchard on the corner of Cambridge Road and Ness Road which I used to climb to get walnuts.

Keith Bailey

BRICKEEN – A LOVELY OLD PLACE

Brickeen was a lovely old place in the High Street, up by Friars Farm. It had a bowling club and a tennis club behind it, with a lovely bowling green and tennis courts. We lived in the High Street and I could look out of my bedroom window and watch the bowling and the tennis matches.

Bob Dack

Friars Farm. Ivy Atkins says, 'Friars Farm was delightful. It was set back from the road with a lovely willow tree behind the front gate.' Friars was purchased by Mrs Snell in 1935; her two daughters married the House brothers and they all lived there together until its demolition in 1973. (Pat Ventris)

Girls celebrating Empire Day, *c.* 1915. Behind them is the waterworks tower in Elm Road, which was built in 1896. The water engineer, Lionel Goodchild, and his family lived in the house on the left and could hear the pumps chugging away all night long. (Margaret Rooke)

WAKERING ROAD – JUST FIELDS

In the 1920s, Wakering Road was mainly just fields. In fact, north of Blackgate Road and Elm Road it was all fields. At Love Lane Cottages there was a shop run by Mrs Jenkins and we called her 'Old Mother Pankerora'. The cottages themselves had been built by Yorkie Ogden and the toilet was out the back, under a big elderberry tree.

George Ventris

ELM ROAD – HANDS ON YOUR HEADS

I was born in Elm Road Cottages. Behind the cottages, Eva, Rose and Walter owned an orchard where the plums were huge and I found them irresistible. Eva would come round to our house and say to my Mum, 'Your Alan's been eating my plums again!'

North of Elm Road there were allotments and cows, birds of every type, including partridges, and adders in the sandpits. Obviously, Elm Road was the site of lots of elm trees and there were loads of bats along there. We used to walk along Elm Road with our hands over our heads because someone had told us that if bats got in your hair you couldn't get them out again.

Over at the brickfields, the night-watchman sat on a pile of bricks. If it rained, the men and their wives and families all had to rush out to cover up the bricks. We used to play over at the brickfields and, when we were older, we smoked wiffey wood [porous dead wood]. If Mr Millbank caught us, he would chase us. He was an athlete who used to run for England.

Earthpit Cottages were just north of Elm Road and were so called because the floors were made of earth. I know one man who lived there whose wife would take him a cup of tea over on the brickfields and would take over the work while he drank his tea. It was all piecework, you see.

The brickfield horses lived in stables on Elm Road and local boys used to go in there and sit on them.

Alan Cundy

RED HOUSE – SECRET TUNNEL

Red House was built as the gatehouse to the Manor House and there is a story that there used to be a tunnel between the two. I know it is true because I know someone who has seen it, but it is bricked up now. Red House originally had a much bigger garden but they sold off some of it and there is now a house and a bungalow built on the garden.

Maureen Clark (née Keys)

CHURCH ROAD – JUST A LITTLE TRACK

I remember Church Road as just a little track with allotments alongside it, with rivulets and creeks running through. There was a football field at the end of Church Road and from Pentland Avenue to Thorpe Bay there was only cornfields. On the right-hand side were malm banks and, over the railway, the brickfields. During the war an AA battery was set up in the malm banks.

Les Dowie

THORPEDENE GARDENS – GOOD ORGANISATION

We lived in Thorpedene Gardens, which was probably the first road to be built on the Thorpedene Estate. I'm told the road was still unmade and remained so for a time. There were many empty plots of land in the road but people who owned these plots had to have all the services put in before the road was made up, so that the road would not be dug up once it was laid (a good bit of organisation).

When we caught diptheria in 1937, we were both carried down to the junction of St Andrew's Road as the ambulance could not get up the road for the mud.

Larry Gains, the boxer, lived a few doors down from us, with his wife and children; Jackie, Harold, Alice and Elizabeth. Larry was a smashing man. We used to hear him in the mornings – the dog would bark and Larry would be padding up the road, going for his run. A lovely family.

Mary Major (née Prime) and John Prime

THORPEDENE – OPEN FIELDS

Before Maplin Way and its surrounds were developed in the 1960s, Caulfield Road ended just beyond Pentland Avenue; between there and Thorpe Bay was just open fields. For access from where I lived in Herbert Road to Thorpe Bay, we used a track which linked Caulfield Road with Station Road. It was a substantial track, wide enough for motor vehicles, although used mostly by pedestrians and cyclists. It was not made-up at all; its surface was just compacted, reddish-coloured clay earth, probably brickearth.

Near the Shoebury end of the track, where it entered Caulfield Road (opposite Connaught Gardens), we sometimes played as children on what we knew as 'marm(y) banks'. These were grass-covered earthen mounds, rather like heavy walls, probably 6ft or so high, enclosing rectangular spaces. These, I now realise, must have been the old brickfield malm banks.

On the southern edge of the Thorpedene Estate there was a footpath crossing Ulster Avenue. This was a lovely tarmacked lane connecting Church Road with Shoebury Cottage and the coastguard station and was known locally as 'Postman's Walk'.

Derek Palmer

Above left: Elm Road, also known as Waterworks Lane. Maureen Clark remembers, 'The last house in Elm Road before the industrial estate was the brickfield manager's house. There was nothing else in the road, not even a light, but I used to ride my bike along there in the dark, no problem, and as children we used to play out in the street in Elm Road. There was no footpath beside the road, just road with trees and bushes all the way along and the brickworks on both sides of the road.'

Above right: Rectory Path, which led from Church Road, past the old rectory, down to Shoebury Common Road. John Prime recalls, 'Shoebury was an idyllic place to live. Down the footpath, on the right-hand side, there was a field of corn with lots of red poppies. Past the cornfield was some scrubland, which became a putting green and beyond that was the boating pond with small boats for hire. Across the road from the boating lake was the car park with beach huts fronting the beach. As well as Uncle Tom's Cabin there was a hut with an opening front where actors put on shows. Before Shoebury Common Road was built, the tide came nearly up to Shore House and there used to be a mooring there for schooners to tie up to while they unloaded on the beach.'

SOMEONE STOLE THE TOILET

In the 1920s, it was like coming into a tiny village, coming up to North Shoebury Post Office along the narrow road from Southend. North Shoebury Road was just a country lane; it was so narrow that the trees almost met overhead. There were just a few black-painted cottages on the Moat House side of the road: the farmworkers' cottages. But North Shoebury was like a foreign country to us. They spoke differently there, with a strong Essex accent. In Wakering they had an even stronger accent and we could hardly understand them – that really was a different country.

When I was a member of the choir I went to some great 'dos' in North Shoebury parish hall, by the old Pyghtle cottage near St Mary's. It was very chummy and I think it was nicer than the new parish hall, even when someone stole the chemical toilet!

Ivy Atkins (née Davis)

THE BEST CHURCH HALL

We went to the Methodist Church in the High Street where Wilhemena Stone played the big pipe organ that had to be pumped with a wooden bar. Dad's job was to do the pumping but he would sometimes doze off and Mrs Stone would kick the organ to wake him up.

The church had two vestries: a minister's and a choir's vestry. Out the back was the church hall and it was one of the best church hall buildings going, with a big kitchen too. Mother used to run a youth club there, which had quite good facilities, such as a snooker table. The hall was very well used, but in the end there was not enough congregation; sometimes it was just Mum and Dad and the minister.

Doreen Penlington (née Gilbey)

The interior of the Methodist Church, High Street. Doreen Penlington says, 'At Harvest festival the smell in the church was wonderful; even the organ was decorated.'
(Peter Owen)

Shoebury High
Street, 1934.
Alan Cundy
remembers,
'When the
top end of the
High Street was
built on Motts
Meadow in the
1920s or '30s,
houses cost
£784 and no
one could afford
them.'
(Peter Owen)

A SPANIEL OUTSIDE

About a dozen soldiers marched up from the garrison to attend the Methodist Church services; they were all very correct and well-behaved. Mr Hopcraft was a superintendent there and I remember watching him pat the butter at his grocers shop.

Fred Cause was the fire chief; he was looked up to and well-respected. His little spaniel used to follow the family up to the Methodist Church and sit outside and wait for them to come out.

Pat Ventris (née Ling)

THE WILLOW PATCH – A SOAKING AND A TELLING OFF

There was a footpath off Elm Road at the side of the water tower where we would cycle up by Millbank's Farm to an area we called the Willow Patch. There were lovely old elm trees there to climb and an old dug-out sandpit, full of wildlife – frogs, toads, waterboatmen, wonderful dragonflies, damselflies of brilliant colours (loads of those), birds and lots of rabbits. It was a smashing place! On the left of the footpath were poles with ropes slung between them to stop gliders landing and when one long length of rope came off and was lying on the ground, my friend John and I transferred it to the Willow Patch and tied it in the elm trees for a swing. We spent a lot of time up there, climbing trees.

Michael Mumford, the son of the postmaster, and I made a raft up there one day but when Michael ventured onto it, it tipped him off into the water. He got a soaking and a telling off and was told not to see me again!

John Prime

CLIMBING TREES AND A HOMEMADE BIKE

We must have climbed every tree in Elm Road. We had to do that because my sister Betty was frightened of dogs so every time we saw a dog she'd say 'Come on, up here!' One time I was halfway down a tree when we saw our dad, a policeman, coming home on his bike and Betty said 'Come on, come on, quick!' and I almost fell down. I got down just in time and we hid in the bushes till Dad rode by and we went home afterwards. We didn't want him to see us because we weren't supposed to be doing that – we were supposed to be young ladies!

One time during the war we made ourselves a bike. We'd always wanted a bike but Dad wouldn't let us have one. We had a den by the allotments near East Beach where we found two bicycle wheels, no tyres on them, and a frame. We managed to put on the wheels so they went round and, me being the youngest, I had to sit on it even though there was no saddle to be wheeled home from Blackgate Road, along the High Street and in the back way up the alley. Of course, it was making a noise and as soon as we got in there Dad looked up from his gardening and said, 'You can take that straight back where it came from!' We were so disappointed; it had taken us about two hours to make.

Margaret Chaplin (née Bates)

Ivy Atkins (*née* Davis) enjoys the fresh air on Elm Road. Behind her is Millbank's Farm and 'Bunkers', a wild area beloved as a playground by many Shoebury children before it was built on in the 1960s. Ivy says, 'When Shoebury Urban District was taken over by Southend Borough [1933], they gave us a little park, Elm Park, with a swing in it. What use was that to us? We would swing off the huge elm trees if we wanted a swing. We had the whole beach and fields to play in; we could walk all the way to Little Wakering without seeing a house. We made our own amusements. It was just wonderful countryside, with lovely flowers.' (Ivy Atkins)

South Shoebury
Common looking
towards the sea, *c.* 1920.

VISITING THE BRICKFIELDS

There was nothing beyond Wakering Road until the Army houses just beyond the border in Wakering. Caulfield Road was a dead end. Delaware Road was just a cinder track, and the bus went up North Shoebury Road to get to Southend as it was the only way to go.

Father used to take me round the Elm Road brickfield on a Saturday morning because he knew people that worked there and he liked to stop and chat. The bricks were all laid out under little shelters to dry out. We'd walk through to the allotments at the back of the brickfields and then in the back way of Grandma's house in Friars Street to visit Grandma.

North of Elm Road was Millbank's farmhouse, called Elm House (Friars School is now on the site). There was a footpath across the fields, just a dirt track then, and there was a sunken field with cows in, belonging to Millbank. When the Council took it on they tried to fill up the sunken field with rubbish to make a rugby pitch but because of the glass, etc, in the rubbish they had a lot of injuries so they couldn't play rugby any more. Now it is the Shoebury Boys' football pitch, but it is still very uneven.

Dad [Lew Keys] used to play football and cricket at the garrison and we would go along and watch him; he also played for Shoebury Town and later Wakering Rovers.

Maureen Clark (née Keys)

BLACKBERRYING ON NESS ROAD

We used to go blackberrying along Ness Road and there was a pond in North Shoebury where my father used to go fishing. There was a good slope where Waterford Road is now where we went tobogganing. Down the bottom there was a boating pool, where the car park is now. We often went swimming too; the seawater was lovely and warm by the evening.

Once a year there was a fair behind the cinema, with stalls like 'shoot the rabbit', rolling coins down a slide, swing boat rides and riding on horses on the carousel.

Joyce Taylor (née Robinson)

The Shoeburyness Hotel, *c.* 1940. Ray Church recalls, 'Jenkins' Garage used to be next to the Shoebury Hotel but it moved to the High Street on the plot of ground where the ARP building, a concrete hut, used to be.'

MEN FOUND OUT

My dad was in the Royal Engineers, so I went to some wonderful children's Christmas parties in the garrison theatre. We also went to the fair behind the cinema, where the Towerfield Estate is now. We once sat on the bridge and watched a man alight dive into a big water tank.

Cripps the Baker of Great Wakering used to come round pulling his cart to deliver bread. He was said to be involved in smuggling, going out to meet the boats. I also remember Miss Mann, who had a shop in Elm Road near the cottages in a side room of her house. She sold wonderful walnut toffee!

They used to call the Shoeburyness Hotel the 'Found Out', because husbands told their wives they were somewhere else but the wives would come in and then they 'found out' where they really were!

Alan Cundy

A VISIT FROM THE QUEEN

An annual event was the visit of the Carnival Queen and her court to Shoebury. I remember the Dagenham Girl Pipers coming too. They would stop outside the Shoeburyness Hotel and then come round the crowds collecting money. It was a big event, very exciting.

The Shoeburyness Hotel, 'The Shoe', was very popular; it was full every night. Next door was Jenkins' Garage, where I used to go to get the wheels of my twin pram aligned – well, hardly anyone had a car so they had the time.

Julia Kalogerides (née Everett)

THREE

School Days

QUEEN OF THE MAY

I was made Queen of the May when I was five years old. My friend was allowed to choose who the Queen would be as a reward for good work. She wanted to choose herself, but she wasn't allowed to, so she chose me, her best friend. Unfortunately, it was bad weather that day and we had to have May Day indoors. They set up the maypole inside and I sat on the teacher's chair. A little boy asked me, 'If you are the Queen, can I be your King?' I think of that as my first proposal!

Empire Day was another big occasion. We all dressed up as different countries and sang songs. I had curly hair and wanted to dress up as a Zulu but Mother wouldn't allow it. She didn't want me to black my face, so I had to be 'Old English' instead. A neighbour made my costume and I wore that costume several times until I grew out of it.

In the winter we liked to make slides on the ice in the playground.

Ivy Atkins (née Davis)

Empire Day at Hinguar Street School, 24 May 1926. Ivy Davis is in the middle row, third from left. (Ivy Atkins)

Empire Day, Hinguar Street School, *c.* 1930. (Pat Ventris)

A TIN FULL OF CHOCOLATE

I started school at Richmond Avenue, but when I reached eleven years old I had to go to Hinguar Street where I stayed until I was fourteen. When it was George V and Queen Mary's Silver Jubilee, every child at Hinguar Street School was given a silver-blue tin filled with chocolate. We took part in the Borough Sports at Jones Memorial Ground where I did high jump and hurdles.

Eileen Whalley (née Scott)

WE WALKED EVERYWHERE

From five years old, we walked from North Shoebury Corner to Richmond Avenue School – well, we walked everywhere, we had no choice. The headmistress, Miss Whitehead, used to be standing out the front of the school in the mornings and you thought she was going to tell you off, but I liked school; my favourite was maths.

On Mondays, my mum would be washing when we went to school and still washing when we came home. We had cold lunch on Mondays or, in winter, a stew.

Iris Lazell (née Wharton)

NEW BOYS TOGETHER

My headmaster was Mr Pountney and I understand that he started at Richmond Avenue School on the same day that I did in 1936, so we were both new boys together! Alice, the daughter of the boxing champion Larry Gains, was in my class.

Dr Paddy Ryan was called to examine my sister who was unwell. It transpired later that she was suffering from TB but the doctor dismissed it, telling my mother, 'You mothers worry too much about your daughters.' She never paid his bill and bore a grudge against him to her dying day.

Ken English

WARTIME EDUCATION

Although I had started school, I wasn't evacuated so my mother taught me spelling and arithmetic while she was doing the housework and looking after a baby sister. It was impossible to buy children's books at this time and the local library never seemed to have more than five children's books at one time. Sometimes there weren't any books at all and I yearned to read.

Left: Miss Cardinal and her staff, Richmond Avenue School, 1930s. (Caroline Gibb)

Below: School play, Richmond Avenue School, 1939. From left to right, the young thespians include: Doreen Scott, Ken English, Jean Dillaway, Derek Farrow, John Finnerty, Enid Sexton, Natalie Hall, Joan Holland, Dave Evans, Geoffrey Haxell, Derek Palmer, Joyce Lipscombe, Pat Harrison, Teddy Lamkin, Peter Morton, Doreen Martin, Gordon Graham and Pat Smith. (Doreen Biles)

After a couple of years some children started to return to Shoebury and Sea View Homes in Ulster Avenue opened as a school. This home was built in the '30s for children whose parents were unable to look after them for one reason or another. (Of course, the children had all been evacuated.) The headmistress was Miss Mann and our wonderful, young, pretty teacher was Miss Mace. There was one other lady teacher who always seemed to be cross. We had coal fires in our classrooms, a nice play area outside and a small piece of woodland where, for most of us, we saw our first squirrel. Although the ages of the children varied greatly, we were well taught. It was a very happy time at school in such lovely surroundings.

We were also encouraged to bring any spare seeds or vegetable plants to school to plant in a vegetable patch for gardening lessons. We always took our gas masks to school with us with our identity number written on the box. I expect everyone still remembers their identity number. Something many of us hated was having our gas mask regularly checked. We put on the mask while an air raid warden held a piece of card over the end. We tried to breathe in and, of course, we couldn't. To get us used to wearing them, my mother would put them on myself and my sister while we helped her to make the beds.

After a while Caulfield Road School, which had been built just before the war as a secondary school, reopened as a primary and secondary school. Most of the teachers were women as the men had been called up. If the air raid siren went off, we had to leave our lessons quietly and go across the playground to the air raid shelters, which were damp and musty. We remained there singing or saying our tables until the 'all clear' siren went off and we returned to our lessons.

Mary Major (née Prime)

Maureen, Sheila and Joyce Rawlings enjoyed four years of education in Derbyshire during the war. (Maureen Andrews)

From left to right: Dennis Smith, Stewart Sutton, Bernard Foster and Frankie Wakefield with Keeper the dog at Castleton, Derbyshire. Dennis Smith says, 'I saw evacuation as a great adventure; I didn't feel homesick at all until we got there.' (Maureen Andrews)

CYCLING TO GREAT WAKERING

During the war there were no schools open in Shoebury so I had to cycle to Great Wakering. I was eight years old, and my sister who came with me was only six. We cycled up Wakering Road, which was a very bare landscape, just a couple of cottages and Love Lane Cottages.

Ron Henn

TWO HOURS A WEEK

Two hours a week in Vincent Crescent is all the schooling I got during the war. After the war I went to Richmond Avenue School where Miss Whitehead had a big, long cane for thrashing boys. I remember her saying, 'I'll break up these gangs!' and thrashing a boy called Tom – he later became a superintendent in the police.

I left school aged fourteen and went to work for Kemsley's, growing tomatoes. When I got home and washed my hair, it was green. Then I became a fitter on the New Ranges and then did my National Service.

Alan Cundy

RAFFIA BASKETS

Because of the war, the first school I went to was Caulfield Road. We had our milk in bottles, which had large, cardboard circles for the tops. During air raids we would join these tops together with raffia to make baskets, while we were sitting down in the shelters. We also spent a lot of time singing 'Ten Green Bottles' and 'One Man Went to Mow' over and over again. At home we had a Morrison table shelter in our living room.

Joyce Taylor (née Robinson)

WATCHING BOMBERS FROM THE PLAYGROUND

During the war, Shoebury was more or less empty apart from the soldiers. I was evacuated to relatives in Wales but soon came back and began school at the Sea View School in Ulster Avenue. From the playground we could see the German bombers going up the Thames, then the siren would go and we would be taken in. From about 1943, people started coming back to Shoebury.

Caulfield Road School was used as an ARP post. Even when it was opened as a school, the ARP had some classrooms and at the end of the school the double oak doors were sandbagged up. It was at Caulfield Road that the 'Cambridge-ites' finally met up with the 'village-ites'.

My teacher was Mr Cardinal; he was a good teacher and he taught me all the way through. In fact, he was even at Hinguar Street when my dad was a boy. He designed his own house in Ness Road and made sure it had bay windows so he had a good view all along Ness Road.

Above left: Hinguar Street School scholarship class, 1935. Pat Ventris (*née* Ling), pictured second from the right, remembers, 'Miss Holmes was my headmistress at Hinguar Street School and my teacher was Miss Merryfield, a little old lady. I was very happy there, until I got to Miss Thomas's class. She took the scholarship class and she used to rap me with a ruler and say, "Behave yourself, Patricia! You'll never pass this scholarship." But my dad said, "You will pass it!" And I did.' (Pat Ventris)

Above right: This photo of the Garrison School football team around 1915, was sent from 'Ernie' to his grandparents, saying, 'On Saturday we rode to Rochford in the garrison wagon and beat them 4-1. We have a good chance now of winning the league.' (Peter Owen)

I went on a school visit to the water tower once and saw how they pumped water from a well. It was lovely water, soft and lathered well. When my grandma and grandad visited from Wales, the first thing Grandad did was drink a glass of water and he would say, 'Beautiful water, that is!'

Tom Ambridge

FLOWERS FOR THE TEACHER

When we came home from being evacuated there was nowhere for me to go to school, although I was five years old by that time. Hinguar Street School was closed and some of the children were being taught at the children's home in Ulster Avenue (now demolished), and others in private houses, but I had to wait for the school to re-open.

I remember my first day as my mother had given me some flowers to take to the teacher (probably to persuade me that I really did want to go). The school had a very dusty feel as it had been closed for quite a while and the only receptacle for my flowers was a jam jar – but they did brighten the place up.

Mr Bowyer was the headmaster at Hinguar Street; he was lovely. My first teacher was Mrs Picken who was marvellous with the young ones. The other teachers I remember are Miss Standon, Miss Gilbey, Mrs Lyons and Miss Thomas, who took the top class. I was in her class when I won the scholarship and went to the Southend High School in Boston Avenue.

When the siren went we all trotted across the playground with our gas mask to the brick air raid shelters and spent a lot of time all sitting round on wooden benches singing 'Ten Green Bottles' and 'One Man Went to Mow'.

We had an Anderson shelter in our back garden and we used to share it with the Edwards family who lived opposite as theirs got flooded.

Margaret Hammond (née Newman)

FROZEN TOILETS

At Hinguar Street School the toilets were in the playground and were completely frozen in the winter. Mr Vernon was the headmaster and was very strict and everyone was frightened of Miss Standon.

Vivienne Odell (née Edwards)

ALWAYS IN TROUBLE

During the war I went to school at the Sea View Homes, later moving on to Richmond Avenue School, which had a completely different atmosphere; it was a proper school. Mr Pountney, who lived in St Andrew's Road, was the headmaster.

Then I moved on to the High School at Caulfield Road, where Mr Napier was the headmaster. One boy in our year came from the Sea View Homes (that is, he was one of the orphans who lived there), and he was always in trouble and always outside Mr Napier's door. At the end of his school life this boy was more than surprised to receive an award at the annual presentation ceremony. Mr Napier announced that the award was 'For someone I got to know quite well, who for all his misdemeanours and problems, has never once been late to school or had a day off.'

I remember school as a fun time; we enjoyed it. We did metalwork, woodwork, gardening and everyone was encouraged to take part. The lessons and the teachers were all quite interesting.

My dad was a Battery Sergeant Major and he bought himself a bright-red bike to get to work saying 'no one will pinch that!' And no one ever did.

Peter Allen

'SAILING' ON BICYCLES

I returned from evacuation to attend Southend High School for Boys. Although, as the school building had been bombed, our classes were initially held at Wentworth Road School. To get to Southend High School we cycled across the Thorpe Bay fields, past the AA gun site. Sometimes we'd get a fright coming back in the afternoon because the soldiers would be getting Bofurs guns ready and they'd let a few rounds off. The shells were held in a clip of five or six and once they started firing, they had to fire all of them. It really gave us a fright – it didn't half rattle!

On Southchurch Boulevard we'd sometimes hang onto the tailboard of a truck to get a free ride up the hard bit.

Coming home in the afternoon it depended on the weather: if there was an east wind we went back the same way, but if the wind was westerly we sometimes went back along the seafront with our coats held open so we could 'sail' along on our bicycles. There was very little traffic then.

Along the seafront at Thorpe Bay was a new 'bungalow'. However, one day I found out it was just a façade; the front of the building dropped down and there was a big gun inside. The bungalow, complete with crazy paved path and birdbath was just to fool any enemy taking photographs; it just looked like a bungalow.

John Prime

LATE FOR SCHOOL

I went to Hinguar Street School where a lot of the Army families went. I remember Miss Dobey, who lived down Cambridge. She was very strict and took the top class of the junior school. Mr Vernon, the headmaster, was an ex-military man and ran the school like it as well!

There was a teacher with a glass eye – Miss Standon. She took the lowest class in the junior school and used to throw chalk and rubbers at you; she was very, very strict.

Hinguar Street School
football team, 1933.
Two teachers with, from
left to right, back row:
Keene, Saxton, Gray,
Evans, Scott. Middle
row: Jewell, Mansfield,
the headmaster,
Woodbridge, Parkins.
Front row: Pitcher.
(Eileen Whalley)

The railway used to go through the village to take the workers to the New Ranges every morning. The train came off Barge Pier, across Campfield Road and across the High Street. The workers used to gather in the High Street at the halt where the train would stop and then it would take the men into the P&EE. They put a gate across the High Street when the train was coming and you had to wait. If you were late for school you couldn't get through the gate and had to wait, so it made you even more late for school.

At Shoebury High School the sports were the best thing. They had tennis courts then, hard ones and lawn tennis, but you didn't get much tennis, we only played in the short summer term. We also played rounders, netball and hockey. The teacher said to me 'Why are you running away from the hockey ball?' 'Because it hurts!' I replied. 'Don't run away, jump over it,' she said. So I started jumping over it, but I got into trouble for that as well.

Maureen Clark (née *Keys*)

WHERE HAVE ALL THE CHILDREN GONE?

Of our class of thirty at Hinguar Street School, there were only about ten kids from Shoebury, the rest of them had parents in the Army. Sometimes they would be posted away overnight, so one day there would be twenty kids missing from the class. We'd come in to school on a Monday morning and there'd only be ten kids, the rest of the class would be gone, left with the Army. It was quite upsetting for a child to have two-thirds of his mates disappear overnight.

Two or three weeks later, another lot would come in. We were ten kids from Shoebury, we were the locals, but these twenty kids from the regiment, they all knew each other – so who were the strangers? We were! Out of the whole lot of kids I started school with at age five, by the time we got to nine or ten, they'd all gone.

I used to go into the garrison quite a bit during the '60s when Mum was working there and I played with Major Lyon's kids in the school holidays. We'd get all our conkers from the trees at the front of Warrior Square and we had a den just inside West Gate – we used to creep in through the hole in the fence.

In the '60s, 36 Regiment had Thunderbird anti-aircraft missiles and where the new road is now was a dummy Thunderbird missile, stood there as a kind of mascot, and they used the Thunderbirds tune as their informal regimental march. They were very supportive of the village and the school in particular.

Last year [2008] I finally got to play cricket in the garrison – I'd wanted to do that since I was a kid!

Trevor Harp

TEA MONITOR

Miss Davy was the headteacher when we started school at Richmond Infants. She ruled with a rod of iron and most people were frightened of her and were on their best behaviour whenever she was about. But she was a very good teacher and became well-known for getting lots of children through the eleven-plus.

There was a teacher (who I thought it best not to name!) who did provide some amusement for the children when she didn't keep her knees together on the teacher's platform at the front of the classroom – we could see her long knickers!

On my first day at Richmond Avenue School I went home at first break time and Mum had to march me back to school. Our nan worked in the kitchens there and in my first few days there I knocked on the door of the kitchen and asked if she would take me to the toilet (the toilets were out in the playground at that time). Miss Davy came up behind me and said 'I'll take you', but I really wanted my nan. However, I got on well and later on I loved school.

Shoebury High School
football team 1954/55.
(Roger Bacon)

Roger Bacon and his brother enjoying the snow outside the Pavilions on Shoebury Garrison during the 1950s. (Roger Bacon)

In my last year at Richmond Avenue I was the tea monitor for Mr Pountney, whose office was upstairs. However careful I was, most of the tea ended up in the saucer so when I got to the top of the stairs I would pour it back into the cup. Mr Pountney never knew and always said what a steady hand I had.

There was an evening club in the High School hall during the '60s, mainly revolving around music. I enjoyed my four years at the High School very much and cried the day I left.

Vivien Pask (née Cox)

YOU! OUTSIDE MY ROOM!

Mr Napier was the headmaster when I started at Caulfield Road in 1951. He was a good headmaster; discipline was 100 per cent. If you were caught talking in assembly it was, 'You, Bacon, outside my room!' Assembly finished and everyone walked by and your face was against the wall. You knew you were going to get the cane and you got it right across your fingertips... but it taught discipline. When Mr Napier left, Mr Mills took over as headmaster. Miss Pilchard was headmistress of the girls' side.

Mr Hagar, the science teacher, lived in Ulster Avenue. Miss Camplin, the art teacher, went to the States and we had this American woman on a year's exchange. When Miss Camplin returned, she married Mr Briggs. I enjoyed my school days.

Roger Bacon

I HATED HOCKEY

At Hinguar Street, Miss Davy frightened me! In needlework we could choose whether to make a dress, a skirt or an apron, and I chose an apron because it was the easiest but Miss Davy said I was lazy.

At the High School I hated hockey; it was always out in the cold and I used to get whacked with the sticks. However, I enjoyed being on the netball team and enjoyed the trampoline.

Norma Tyler (née Cox)

LESSONS IN THE AIR RAID SHELTER

A few years ago I decorated Hinguar Street School and found it was set out exactly the same as it was when I was there. Teachers I remember are Miss Dobey, Miss Thomas, who taught the last year, and Miss Standon, who went with the children who were evacuated during the war. My dad wouldn't let us be evacuated, so we had a lot of our lessons down in the school air raid shelter.

At the High School I enjoyed the gardening lessons very much. Every class had its own allotment on the right-hand side of the school building and we grew all sorts of vegetables, which were used for school dinners.

An outing to Trafalgar Square for pupils of Shoebury High School, *c.* 1952. (Robert Dack)

Headmaster Mr Mills (centre) with pupils of Shoebury High School, March 1956. (Roger Bacon)

Some of my teachers at the High School were Mr Hedges, Mr Aspinall, the games teacher, Mr Melverton, the metalwork teacher, Miss Danks, the art teacher, and Mr Strong. If you could get Mr Strong talking about the war you could get out of having to do the maths lesson! Mr Napier was the headmaster who was strict but fair. He wore a black gown and mortarboard.

I was at school when King George died. I was out on the sports field and someone came over and said 'The King has died.'

I wonder if everyone remembers the Shoebury High School song?

> All men must be free
> March for liberty with me.
> Brutes and braggarts may have their little day
> We shall never bow the knee.
> God is drawing His sword,
> We are marching with the Lord
> Sing then brother, sing, giving everything.
> All you are and hope to be
> To set the peoples free.

Bob Dack

DANCING WITH MR STRONG

Mr Pountney was my first headmaster. Teachers I remember at Shoebury High School include Mr Cardinal and Mr Strong. Once a week after school, Mr Strong taught us dancing. We'd all stand in a line and try to follow the steps; it was popular with the boys as well as girls. I've always loved dancing.

Doreen Biles (née Scott)

FOUR

Out and About

BLEAK BY THE COASTGUARDS

In my day, the boys were either 'village' or 'Cambridge'. Cambridge boys would get duffed up if they came into the village area, but if we knew that boys from Great Wakering were coming, we'd join forces against them.

The area behind the Bug Hutch was called 'Freezers', named for Mr Frost who worked there as an odd job man. There were allotments there and all the way up to Vincent Crescent.

It could be bleak down by the old coastguard station. Before the road was made up there were just grassy cliffs from Shoebury Common and along to Thorpe Bay corner and they put a rope along the edge as a guide for people coming along in the dark, so they didn't fall off.

Tom Ambridge

CHEESE AND MUSTARD SANDWICHES

Bunkers was wild. We made rope swings and built dams over there. The pond that's now in Friars Park used to be huge and there was another pond off Elm Road belonging to Millbank's where we used to make rafts and get up to all sorts. We'd go over the brickfields and push the trucks around and sometimes we got chased off.

There was a grocers opposite the railway where we could get a penny apple or a couple of walnuts to take to school with us. The Co-op baker, Mr Bearman, used to come round with his cart. He sold cheese and mustard sandwiches and always used to give me one. We had Dr Dockery but I didn't go there very often, we just went to Mr Cordon the chemist. He'd even take the fish hooks out of my fingers.

David Odell

MARBLES IN THE GUTTER

The Drabbies used to come along with the horses every morning. They used to come up from the garrison stables to work on the farms, sometimes with the Army carts. There was a pig farm on the left of Wakering Road and the military horses used to work on it. Behind the farm was

Shoeburyness coastguard station, actually just across the boundary in Thorpe Bay and now the site of the Thorpe Bay Yacht Club.

an area we used to call 'Bunkers'. It was part of the brickfields but we used to go over there all the time to play. Now it is the Painters Estate. We also used to play over Shoebury Park and the Ten Range behind East Beach (so called because it had ten sheds on it).

We played football by the malm banks, and marbles in the gutter in the High Street. Dr Ryan had a car and the newsagent had a car; I think they were the only cars in the High Street. We could go over the garrison when we wanted except one day a year when they closed it so it didn't become a public right of way.

Bob Dack

BOY SCOUTS

One day a Mr Robinson came to see my parents and said, 'Would your son be interested in helping set up a Scout group, because I'm thinking of setting one up?'

So we set up the 4th Shoeburyness Scout Troop with Mr Jupp as the scoutmaster. We met at the Methodist Church in St Andrew's Road where Mr Robinson had just built the new hall. We went to the youth club there too – the attraction of that was that girls went there too. That was run by Jim Hurst, who was very good.

The Scouts had parade once a month when it was an honour to carry the flag, walking from Linton Road to the church. I was the youngest one to get my Queen's Scout. I enjoyed getting my pioneer's badge too. For that you had to make a bivouac out of twigs and leaves in Southchurch Park and you slept in it overnight and then skinned and prepared a wood pigeon.

Uncle Tom's Cabin is where the Scouts would go for outside recreation and have a campfire or do certain tests to qualify for the 2nd or 1st Class stage of Scouts. We also lived out at Millbank Farm, Elm Road, where the football pitch is now (and underneath that, a Council tip). It was all scrubland there then; none of that was built on. We used to do tracking in there and we used to make campfires down at the coastguard on the car park there, where the boat lake used to be. I used to walk to Belchamps in Hawkwell from Shoebury for Scout camp. We all walked everywhere – until you got a bicycle.

Roger Bacon

A LOAD OF HOOLIGANS

I went to the 2nd Shoebury Scout Troop in Dane Street where Lionel Pollard was the scoutmaster. We were the biggest load of hooligans in the area and had great fun with our staves, axes and sheath knives! We had treasure hunts on East Beach and went camping at Belchamps.

The sandpits behind the Bug Hutch were a playground for us. We used to come out of the cinema and carry on the film in our games, cowboys and Indians, or Tarzan, for example. Another favourite play area was the brickfield and another was what is now Friars Park.

But it wasn't all play. I was a paper boy for Burrows and a choir boy at St Peter's in a starched collar and surplice and cassock. The choir was led by two ladies who ran a haberdashery shop during the week. One was a tiny lady who played the organ and the other kept us in order.

Dennis Smith

Left: Shoeburyness Common, the site of many of the Scouts' outdoor activities. (Peter Owen)

Below: The 4th Shoeburyness Scout Group, 1950s, outside their headquarters, the Methodist Chapel in St Andrew's Road. Note the absence of the church hall. (Roger Bacon)

The 4th Shoeburyness Scout Troop, 1950s, away on camp. (Roger Bacon)

THE MERRYMAKERS

Mrs House lived at Friars Farm with her husband and children, Pat and David. She used to be on the stage and she started a drama group called The Merrymakers, which I went to from about the age of five; lots of children used to go. We'd do sketches, songs, plays and tap dancing; I loved it! The shows were very popular; in fact, we put on three shows every year at St Peter's hall, in the garrison theatre which burnt down and at the Band of Hope hall in North Shoebury. We practised in St Peter's church hall and Mum used to make us the clothes.

Doreen Penlington (née Gilbey)

COLD IN THE HALLS

Everyone belonged to The Merrymakers. Mrs House made most of the costumes herself, but some of them were very cold, particularly when we were changing for shows in the halls! We practised on Friday nights at St Peter's church hall in the High Street and travelled around Shoebury to do shows. Singing, dancing, acting – we did it all. Mrs House was very strict and we had to be very disciplined, but it was our life; there wasn't much else to do. On the way to practices I was allowed to pop into the off-licence in the High Street to buy a packet of crisps. They hadn't long been invented.

Vivienne Odell (née Edwards)

PROUD TO BE A FAIRY

I joined The Merrymakers when I was about five years old. It was run by Mrs House, who wrote all the plays and songs herself as well as making most of the costumes. The shows were a big event; everyone went. I was very proud to get the part of a fairy one year. Mrs House needed someone who could read joined-up writing and my friend said, 'Julia can read', and so I got the part.

Julia Kalogerides (née Everett)

Above left: The Merrymakers, *c.* 1950. Many girls (and a few boys) have happy memories of Mrs House's Merrymakers entertainment troop. (Vivienne Odell)

Above right: Methodist Church, Shoebury High Street. Built in 1893, it was the scene of many church service, Sunday school and youth club memories. (Peter Owen)

HALLELUJAH!

We lived next door to the Salvation Army hall – so we knew all the songs! The noise! There was only one wall dividing us. 'Onward Christian Soldiers' – I used to find myself singing the songs at work. They had band practice in that hall too; luckily it was a good band. One good thing about the Salvation Army was the Sunday school outings, to Maldon, for example, or Walton. I also went on trips with the Eagle Club, which was a working men's club in Sea View Road. They had loads of coaches taking us all out on day trips.

Keith Bailey

ST ANDREW'S YOUTH CLUB

Mrs Cook, the wife of the butcher whose shop was on the corner of George Street, started a youth club at St Andrew's Church in 1946. She was a remarkable woman, a real pioneer.

We got involved with all sorts of things. For example, we once cooked a meal – hot meat pies – for over 100 old people. During the holidays we used to go on cycle rides, to Canewdon or Hullbridge, for example. It was great!

We had a beach hut on East Beach and we did campfire cooking at Bunkers, the area north of Elm Road. We also put on concerts and had parties.

Joyce Taylor (née Robinson)

SACK RACES, SOUP AND GLOOPY MUD

We went on Sunday school outings to Elm Road park, which was a very rural area; there was nothing in Elm Road but Millbank's meadow and farm. We'd take a picnic and we'd have sack races and other racing games. It was a good afternoon out.

I nearly drowned my little sister in the pond once. And I cut her hair. She had lovely, long hair and it was my job to put it up in rag papers, winding it round and round. I hated it so I said to her, 'Would you like me to cut your hair?' and she said 'Yes', so I cut it off.

On the brickfields we used to play amongst the bricks and kilns and we smoked wiffey wood and built dens. The malm banks at East Beach were full of gloopy mud, but we would run round the top of them all the time, oblivious to any danger.

Beyond the black huts in Wakering Road there was a pig farm and a rope swing on the trees up there. Jenkins' sweet shop was down Love Lane and their cat used to lay all over the sweets – but we still ate them.

In 1936 there was a strike and Councillor Cause and his wife ran a soup kitchen and we went with a big jug to get soup for our dinners from his big house on the corner of the High Street.

Joy Bateman (née Gilbey)

SUNDAY SCHOOL AND YOUTH CLUB

Sunday school was at the Mission Hall in Wakering Avenue, led by the Levett family. Each year we would be taken to Theydon Bois for the summer outings, for a picnic, races and games.

In the 1950s Fred Hodges was one of the leaders of the Methodist youth club which was held in the big hall at the back of the church two or three nights a week; lots of children went to play table tennis and games.

Maureen Andrews (née Rawlings)

Young equestrians from the Garrison Riding School around 1955 in front of the Drill Shed, including Julia Kalogerides (*née* Everett), second from right. (Julia Kalogerides)

PROJECTIONIST AT THE PALACE

You could go dancing down in the barracks if you were going out with a soldier – but I only loved sailors. I didn't like the cinema either when I was a little girl, I was frightened to death. But my brother, Frank, was the first projectionist at the Palace Cinema. That was his first job and he was ever so little; they asked him if he wanted a stool to stand on.

Iris Lazell (née Wharton)

CINEMAS AND FAIRS

The Palace Cinema was another attraction, 6*d* I think, and behind the cinema a fair would arrive annually with swing boats, chairs on planes and all sorts of attractions. There was plenty of noise from the organ playing and the steam engine driving the merry-go-round.

Mary Major (née Prime)

I'LL STOP THE FILM!

The Palace Cinema had several managers over the years. One I remember was a dapper little man who was at the pay desk, took your money and when you passed through to the auditorium was already there waiting to take the ticket he had just given you and to show you to your seat. He would then reappear at frequent intervals with other patrons – he appeared to be everywhere, rather like a pinball! When the first film finished he appeared again, this time with a tray of ice cream. He seemed to perform every duty; I have an idea he was also the projectionist.

Shoeburyness
Silvertown Band.
(Colin and Gillian
Blackall)

Above left: Ness Road, with the Palace Theatre (Bug Hutch) far right. John Askew remembers, 'If you got to the cinema before two o'clock on a Saturday you could get in for 2*d*. That's why there was what we called the 'tuppenny rush', just before two o'clock.'

Above right: The Cambridge Hotel, Ness Road, remembered as always being full of holidaymakers and young soldiers, and for its lively dances.

When he left his place was taken by a lady who took no nonsense at the Saturday kid's shows. She was very tall and bony and heron-like and, if the kids were unruly, she would shout at the top of her voice 'If you're not quiet, I'll stop the film!' I remember two occasions when she was true to her word, the lights went up, the picture faded out and the sound gradually came to a halt! Despite this, I spent many happy hours in the Bug Hutch. If you hadn't any money, you could always sit on the seat in Campfield Road and listen to the soundtrack!

Dave Evans

CRUNCHY PEANUTS

In the cinema, if the projectionist dozed off and forgot to change the reel in the middle of the film the numbers would come up on the screen: 9, 8, 7, 6, 5. On Saturday mornings they showed cowboy and adventure films but I liked the Charlie Chaplin films. Everyone seemed to have crunchy peanuts and it was very noisy in there. The school sometimes showed films in the evenings too.

Joyce Taylor (née Robinson)

DILAPIDATED SEATS

Oh, yes, I remember the Palace Theatre. Mr Alexander was the cinema owner. My dad loved the cinema and would often take me, sometimes twice a week. I would sometimes go by myself after school on a Wednesday and on a Saturday with Dad. If it was a cowboy film, Dad's sister, Kathleen, would take us, walking over the step bridge behind the cinema, but she only liked the cowboy films.

The box office was in the middle of the entrance and then you would go in either side. I never went upstairs – we couldn't afford it! Downstairs the seats were so dilapidated that you could take the arms off and lie down along the seats, but it got quite full on a Saturday. After the film we would buy an ice cream next door and take the bus home.

Maureen Clark (née Keys)

LOOKING FOR TROUBLEMAKERS

Mrs Caron, the manageress of the Palace Cinema, used to come round with her torch looking for troublemakers. Mr Drury was the next manager; he didn't stand any nonsense either. There were lots of soldiers in there because it was cheap. When seats got broken in the cinema they would just take them out so you'd try to sit down in the dark and find a gap! There was one film on Monday, Tuesday, Wednesday, then they'd change the programme for Thursday, Friday and Saturday. We came out on Saturday mornings from the cinema and went up the lane to Freezers and had stone fights and all sorts.

Tom Ambridge

The Waterloo Road entry for the Southend Carnival. (Doreen Biles)

A LONG WALK HOME

Shoeburyness was the most beautiful place to be brought up. We used to walk to the park on Elm Road and play on the swings, roundabout and see-saw. It was really lovely. Sometimes I'd use my brother's skates, tied up with string.

As teenagers, me and my friend Betty went to the garrison NAAFI every Friday night to dance to the live band. Once a month they had dances at the gym on Campfield Road too. Of course, it was full of soldiers but there was never any trouble there.

We also liked to go roller-skating at the Gliderdrome on the seafront. It was fantastic! I remember the butcher from the shop in Ness Road who would be there doing all the fancy steps with his wife.

The Shoebury cinema was known as the Bug Hutch. There were three films a week: one on Sunday, then another on Monday, Tuesday and Wednesday and then a third on Thursday, Friday and Saturday. I went as often as I could. My brother had a friend in the projection office, so we went in there sometimes. I even acted as the usherette and helped in the pay box.

The buses were so busy! To go to Southend, we would sometimes take the bus going in the opposite direction to Shoebury Village and then get on the Southend-bound bus there, because it was easier than trying to get on in Cambridge Town.

One year, my sister and I dressed as Hawaiian girls for the Waterloo Road entry in Southend Carnival. When we walked up the cliffs to collect money some people got their matches out and joked that they would set fire to our grass skirts. It was fun… but then our lorry broke down and we had a long walk home!

Doreen Biles (née Scott)

ALLOTMENTS AND WATERWORKS

Before the war we used to dig earth out of the ditches behind the cinema, alongside Grove Walk. It was beautiful earth and people would buy it for their allotments.

When Shoebury was taken over by Southend [1933] they sold our waterworks, which they had no right to do. The water from the Shoebury waterworks was so soft; it was beautiful. It was said to come from an underground river all the way from Norway.

Les Dowie

TREASURES FROM CHICK'S SCRAPYARD

From Chick's scrapyard I got four wheels and axles and made a trolley. I took it down to the front to collect driftwood and for collecting seaweed in sacks for Dad's allotment.

Then I bought two long-range aircraft fuel tanks and made a boat with Dad's help as, having been an electrician and engineer, he had all the tools. That was our first boat and my friend John and I took it out to the Mulberry Harbour.

Then we bought an old dinghy for £1 10s, scrounged some pitch and some old powdered-milk tins and patched it up. The sail was made out of barrage balloon material from Chick's.

John Prime

HIGHLIGHT OF THE WEEK

Dancing in the gymnasium on Campfield Road on a Thursday night was the highlight of the week. We once went to a sergeants' ball where they had a pig's head with an apple in its mouth. Everyone was all dressed up: the soldiers were in their blue uniforms, their evening dress uniforms. I think it was held in the gymnasium too.

We walked miles in them days. Thought nothing of walking from Southend to Shoebury – we'd come out of the pictures and just walk home. However, when I started work in Southend I used to cycle, puffing and blowing up Southchurch Boulevard. Sometimes I went on the bus; it was 5d for a workman's return.

June Edwards

MEMORIES OF NAN

We used to walk through the barracks on our way to visit our nan. If you walked down Campfield Road there were loads and loads of soldiers crossing the road from the barracks to get to the gymnasium and the NAAFI.

Our nan lived in 'old Shoebury' in John Street in a two-up, two-down. Actually, it was really three-up because there was a third room you could get to through one of the others. Auntie Minnie lived on the corner of Rampart Street and Uncle Arthur a little further down in very similar houses.

Nan's front door opened straight into the front room, but we never used that room; it was for high days and holidays only. I remember the fox wrap on the back of the chaise longue Nan had in there. Then there was the middle room with the range in it; this is where the family ate. The back room had the kitchen sink. Right out the back was the wash house and the outside loo.

Every Monday Nan would start boiling the copper to get ready for washing. She was washing all morning, then would put it all through the mangle and in the afternoon get it all dried. For wet days she had one of those airers that hangs from the ceiling.

Nan used to send me out with a jug to get some beer from the Shoeburyness Hotel for Grandad. Nan herself had a Guinness every morning at eleven o'clock with some fresh bread and cheese – that was her mid-morning snack.

Sometimes Nan would send me round to Jackson's with the empty ginger beer bottles and with the money I got back on the empties, I could get a new bottle. When I got back to the house with it, Nan would send me out again to get bread. Why she couldn't send me to two places at once I don't know, but she never did.

Vivien Pask (née Cox)

Left: Young gentlemen outside the conveniences on East Beach prom, late 1940s. From left to right: Jack Amos, Peter Errington, Tony McHugh and Dennis Smith. (Ron Henn)

Below: Jeff's Café, pictured from East Beach. (John Wenning)

RABBITING WITH GRANDAD

My grandad kept ferrets for rabbiting and had a pass to catch rabbits in the garrison and New Ranges. He would go over there with my dad, Tony Glasscock, George Bracey (in his leather leggings) and his dogs. He loved nothing better. The ferrets were quite affectionate with Grandad, but I was not allowed to handle them.

George Ventris

FIVE

Beaches, Holidays and Holidaymakers

ALWAYS HOT AND SUNNY

I reminisce of the hot, sunny days; I forget the winters with no central heating, etc… but were not all the days hot and sunny in the 1940s and '50s? We used to walk out on the mud for a mile or so, no harm ever came to us and at the end of the day the man who owned the shop on the beach would organise us into picking up the rubbish from the beach and having a bonfire. Mr Kay was his name; he also owned the photographic shop in Smith Street and, later, the High Street.

Gloria Burwell (née Everett)

HUNDREDS OF VISITORS

Mother would take in visitors during the summer. Several people did as there were not enough lodgings for everyone. My sister and I slept on our parents' bedroom floor and the visitors had our bedrooms. We didn't mind. During the day, if the visitors had children, it was our job to take them out and entertain them.

In the summer we tried to go to the beach on a Monday because the trippers came down from London on a Saturday and Sunday to sit on the beach and their coins would fall out of their pockets. So on a Monday, we went searching for any coins we could find.

Sawkins the blacksmith was on East Beach, where the bus shelter is now. My parents lodged with the Sawkins family when we first came to Shoebury, so we knew them quite well and used to go down to watch the horses getting new shoes.

A troop of entertainers called The Jolly Boys used to perform on Cambridge Beach.

Ivy Atkins (née Davis)

SWIMMING, SEAWEED AND BOATS

I was brought to Shoebury to visit my grandparents from a very young age and visits usually involved taking me to the beach. There were cliffs all along East Beach to the MoD land, but the cliffs were gradually knocked down by the brickfield work. I remember the big kilns on the East Beach brickfields, and the 100ft-long piers stretching out to the barges moored out beyond the mud. The barges would come alongside the piers and the 'brickies' had to run along the pier with their barrowload of bricks and unload the bricks onto the barges.

My uncles Harry, Bill and Sid were very good swimmers and one day when I was about seven, I announced that I would like to learn to swim like them. So, Uncle Harry took me to the end of one of these piers and threw me in! And that's how I learned to swim.

At the end of Rampart Street was a forge where the children would gather round to watch the horses being shod. Behind the beach, where Dane Street now is, was a pig farm and my friend collected seaweed for the pigs' feed. We also used to collect seaweed and take it to the chemist where people would buy it to put in their bath – it was apparently very good for arthritis. We were very organised; all the children would collect the seaweed and then some of the older boys would take it to the chemist and sell it for us.

As a young man, I worked on the boats which would take people out for trips, up to the pier for example. There were ten or twelve boats working from Shoebury. I remember the *Duchess of York*, the *Prince of Wales* and the *Skylark* on West Beach. There were lots of boats for hire from Mason's boathouse under the coastguard station, but I never heard of one casualty. I rented out boats for fishing trips and looked after the rowing boats. We had to push down the landing stage according to the state of the tide. If people didn't come back in quick enough, they got stuck on the mud, so they'd put down the anchor and walk back to shore. That meant someone had to go out to collect the boats as soon as the tide came in – sometimes it meant getting out there at 4 a.m.!

I was working on the *Prince of Wales* helping people into the boat on the day war was declared. It was a very nice day. As I was in the first aid brigade, a man came down to find me and said, 'Get your uniform on, war has been declared.' The boat emptied immediately and the owner was not best pleased!

Children photographed on Shoebury Common Beach in 1926. Ivy Atkins says, 'There were hundreds of visitors. It was easier for them to get to the beach from Shoebury Station than to get off in Southend and walk down the cliffs, so they came to Shoebury.' (Eileen Whalley)

Above left: Rampart Terrace. Ray Church remembers, 'There were two huts on the prom, which made great goal posts. We often played football between them.' (John Wenning)

Above right: Shoebury Hall caravan site, owned by Captain and Mrs Townend. Les Dowie says, 'The site was beautifully kept; very smart.' (Peter Owen)

Above left: Uncle Tom's Cabin, *c.* 1935. Mary Major says, 'Uncle Tom's Cabin was a wonderful stop: buckets, spades and beachballs were plentiful, together with sweets and ice creams. I can still recall the smell inside the building.' (Peter Owen)

Above right: Shoebury boating lake. Mary Major remembers, 'The boating lake beside the putting green was certainly there before the war and cost 6d.'

Lots of boys from Hinguar Street went into the Royal Artillery, quite a few boys from my era. Their names are now on the cenotaph.

After the war I took a job at Horndon-on-the-Hill and cycled there and back from Shoebury every day.

Les Dowie

SHOEBURY HALL CAMPSITE

I remember the Shoebury Hall campsite as being very clean. When it first opened there were just tents, but later there were caravans. My husband used to come down for holidays with a friend's family and camp for the whole summer. His friend came into the shop where I worked one day and went back and told Ken, 'There's a nice blonde girl working in there'. After that, Ken kept coming into the shop (Griffiths in Ness Road) to buy things.

Mother took in holidaymakers during the summer for bed and breakfast. Everybody did. If we didn't have room we'd pass them on to the neighbours. Many of them became good friends and would take us out with them and they would come back to stay with us every year.

Doreen Biles (née Scott)

SUMMER DAYS

The caravan park was a huge site, right up to the Shore House. Near the Shore House was a big boat lake where you did the old paddles, you know, the wind ones. It was hard work!

We often went swimming during the summer off Shoebury Common, where Leitrim Avenue comes down. I used to work in the morning during the holidays, for example smashing up the old air raid shelter for my dad and doing a Saturday morning job at Parkins' greengrocers in the High Street, almost opposite Smith Street. I used to cook their beetroots and sort out their cabbages to be put in the front of the shop. When Mother bought eggs from Parkins she always cracked them into a cup first, because if you got a bad one you could take it back and get a replacement.

Roger Bacon

Jack and Eileen Scott with friends enjoying Shoebury Common Beach during the 1920s. (Doreen Biles)

Above: East Beach, with the beach huts, most of which were destroyed in the 1953 floods. George Ventris says, 'Years ago, the bargees would lay their sails on the beach to dress them. They kept the barges nice and my mother had to take her shoes off to go on them.'

Left: Keith Bailey, front centre, and his family and friends enjoying a day on Shoebury Common Beach, *c.* 1949. 'I love the place,' says Keith. 'I wouldn't live anywhere else.' (Keith Bailey)

DOWN TO THE SHORE

There was a footpath (now Waterford Road) which ran down from Church Road to the seafront. On the left was the caravan site owned by Captain Townend. This was quite busy during the summer. At the bottom of the footpath was wasteland, consisting of brambles and gorse; the Shore House came much later. We collected a piece of gorse bush each year and used it as a Christmas tree. On the right-hand side (i.e. west) was a putting green, which, I think, was made there after the war. The boating 'lake' beside it was certainly there before the war. We often used both of these facilities – *6d* on the boating lake.

After the war the beach reopened. Lots of rabbits had burrowed under the beach huts but soon disappeared once people began to use the beach again. We had wonderful days on the beach with our picnics. Everything tasted wonderful eaten in the fresh air. Of course, food was still rationed for many years to come. We didn't have holidays; we didn't need them. We collected cockle shells from the beach, painted and varnished them and made them into necklaces. We collected twigs and decorated them with pieces of glitterwax, which had a slight perfume and we thought they looked really pretty.

Mary Major (née Prime)

WINCHING UP THE BOATS

There were two boats working from Shoebury Common Beach that would take day trippers out to the estuary for rides around the pier or out to the wrecked Mulberry Harbour. Each boat could take up to thirty persons.

My husband, John, then aged about sixteen, together with his friend, (also) John, worked to help the skippers during their holidays. The work involved pushing the boats down the beach as the tide receded, then winching them up again as the tide 'made' again. For this enjoyable labour they were rewarded with a few shillings, which were spent at the kiosk near the beach. This kiosk sold all kinds of goodies including toffee apples, which the two Johns helped to make during the boats' periods out at sea. They also collected cockles when the tide was out and would boil them in Mum's boiler and put them in jars of vinegar to sell.

Joyce Taylor (née Robinson)

JUMPING OFF THE JETTIES

There were three or four jetties from East Beach to load the barges with bricks. They were good for jumping in the water from, but you had to be careful because there were clumps of old bricks under the water where they had been dumped. I cut my head once and a policeman carried me home, from where I was taken to the military hospital.

Dennis Smith

FISHING MEMORIES

We used to put a fishing line out, me and my younger brother, Ian. We pegged a length of line and off of that main line, a line with about 500 hooks and leave it till the tide came in. Then you had to follow the tide out because if the water was less than 6ft the seagulls would get the fish. On a good day we might get a Dover sole or something like that, which we'd take to the fish shop for pocket money.

Above left: The *Duchess of York* setting off from Shoebury Common Beach with a boat load of trippers. (Peter Owen)

Above right: John and Mary Prime on Shoebury Common Beach with their parents, *c.* 1935. (Mary Major)

There used to be a load of local boats and the owners set up the Shoebury Watermen's Association. The first time I fished out on the boats I was aged only about eight or nine, but I caught eleven fish that day. I got a lovely Dover sole and Tommy Church offered me eight bob for it – that was a lot of money, beyond my wildest dreams – but I said 'No, it's the first fish I've caught. I'm going to keep it'.

The best fishing was off the Old Ranges (Dad got a 27lb cod once) and the best cockles were collected off the Officers' Mess, so we sometimes had a run-in with the War Department coppers. We'd go straight out from the beach and then across to the Army land. However, by the time they'd seen us, got their boots on, got the dog out the van and got out to us, we'd have come back in.

A lot of people in Shoebury maintain that they still have commoners' rights over the fishing grounds but the Army disagrees. So there's always been a bit of a battle here.

Trevor Harp

COME HOME WHEN THE SIREN GOES

From the age of about ten I was allowed to go down to the beach alone. I used to cycle down in my swimming costume with a plastic mac on top. I'd leave my bike and have a swim and then just put my plastic mac on and cycle home. I didn't take a towel, I'd get dry at home.

When my cousins came here on holiday we played cricket on the mud; we'd spend hours down there. We'd jump off the boom into the water, but we weren't allowed to go out on the mud when the tide was coming in as it was too dangerous. Once we collected cockles in our swimming costumes, all stuffed inside. Of course, they were woolly costumes so they were really sagging, and we had buckets full too. We got them home and Dad put them in a galvanised bucket on the stove but then he said, 'I don't like the look of these cockles' and he wouldn't let us eat any of them; he threw them away, so all our cockle collecting was just a waste.

Behind the beach we would pick wildflowers on the site of the old brickfield. The car park is there now. There were trees where the entrance to the MoD is now and trees along Peel Avenue, where we used to take ropes and make swings. There was a farmhouse where the track for the railway goes across by the MoD entrance.

The Army owned East Beach from the barracks up to where the toilet block is now and we weren't allowed to use that part of the beach. We used to get to it from the middle of the High Street through the old coal yard and across the railway line. The Army had huts on what is now the car park, where they used to work, and they had corrugated iron shelters and iron Nissen huts that had plant, lorries and trucks in them.

When we were playing by the beach, we could always tell the time by the *Royal Daffodil* coming past. It went to France twice a week and also went to Margate. It would leave the pier at ten o'clock and pass us about lunchtime, so we knew what the time was. When it came back it was time to go home.

We could also tell the time by the sirens for the Ranges workers. They started work at half past seven, so a siren would sound at 7.20 a.m. Another siren at twelve o'clock notified lunchtime, and then the last siren was at half past four, when they used to leave work. My mum used to say, 'Come home when the siren goes.'

Maureen Clark (née Keys)

LOTS OF ACCIDENTS

On Saturday and Sunday evenings you could not get onto East Beach for the masses of cars coming off it – a continuous stream of traffic. I belonged to the St John Ambulance and used to work down at the beach at the weekends. We did our training at St Peter's church hall and you had to do so many hours 'work' to get your badges. There would be two adults and two girls working at a time on East Beach and we had people coming to us all the time with cuts and bruises; there were lots of accidents.

There were many pleasure boats that used to go out, including two or three from East Beach. They put a plank of wood on a box to load people and I used to jump on. The boats were 20-30ft long with seats around and they'd take people out for half-hour trips or for fishing trips.

Vivienne Odell (née Edwards)

GET 'EM WET

As kids we lived down East Beach. We had a boat down there and we four brothers would give boat trips. We put up a board to advertise and had plenty of customers. We'd take them a mile or so out or round the barracks – 'get 'em wet and fetch 'em back', we'd say. In the 1940s it was 3*d* or 6*d* for a trip; in the '50s and '60s it was a 1*s* or 2*s*.

Ray Church

Left: John Taylor watches the *Skylark* off Shoebury Common Beach, 1948. (John Prime)

Below: John Church, seen here with some young relatives, was a foreshore inspector and his department was allowed £500 a year for clearing old bricks off East Beach during the late 1960s. (Ray Church)

POCKET MONEY FOR RIDES

The beach was a favourite for us. We made a swing out of rope tied to a branch of a huge elm tree and took turns to run along the bank and swing out over the smaller trees. We also used to search the rubbish bins after the day trippers had gone home to look for returnable bottles to take to the off-licence in the High Street to get money for sweets and pocket money for rides on the *Pride and Joy*, skippered by Des Church.

We built dens in stacks of bricks in the brickfield, played over the fields and went fishing over at Bunkers, where we also picked blackberries and mushrooms in the autumn. During the summer school holidays, some of us helped my mum and my aunts on Millbank's Farm, potato and pea picking to get pocket money.

Brian Kane

FANTASTIC TIMES

My mother would meet me from Richmond Avenue School with a bag of sandwiches, a flask of tea and my swimming costume and we would go straight down to the beach, where Dad would join us after work. If the tide was in we would swim; if the tide was out we would go cockling – they were great days.

At low tide, horses from the Shoebury Garrison would gallop along the shore, almost to the pier and back. They were in pairs with a soldier riding one horse and leading another beside him.

I remember Thames barges from Woolwich sailing up to Barge Pier on the garrison beach. It was lovely to see them sailing past Shoebury Common Beach, a wonderful sight. If there was an easterly wind it was extremely difficult for the sailing barges to get out of the Thames mouth against the tide and wind, so they would all wait in the Medway and come out in a stream when the wind changed.

Before the war, I learned to sail and row in the rowing boats owned by Percy Robinson and the sailing boat, *Kitty,* owned by Jack Robinson. For some reason, he used to play records on the boat on a wind up gramophone and I used to wind it up. They were fantastic times… and it never rained.

Stan Goulding owned the *Skylark* and the *Prince of Wales* and we'd help him too. Whatever he said, we'd do; look after his landing stage and help with the occasional trip out, for example.

My friend John and I used to row out to the Mulberry Harbour, occasionally doing a bit of fishing, sometimes catching 'flatties' – flounders and plaice. When the tide came in, we'd come back.

John Prime

HUNDREDS OF BRICKS

Every Saturday there was a game of football off George Street from about half past nine in the morning. All the lads from the school would wander over at various times and join in; they'd come along one or two at a time until there was about ten of us on each team. We'd all go home for lunch about twelve when the score was about 26-24 and come back and be down there until it was dark. The score would be something like 36-32!

When we were kids we could walk into the sea at East Beach and find it was just bricks for about 20yds out, hundreds and hundreds of bricks. You literally had to struggle to get over them and if you dived in off the jetty you had to be careful you didn't cut yourself. They were left over from when the barges used to come up and a lot of bricks used to go over the side and were just left there. They once had a load of volunteers come down to pick most of the bricks up. The local lads never, ever went in the water in bare feet; you could always tell who the 'outsiders' were – they had bare feet.

Trevor Harp

A LOT OF LONDONERS

During the summer holidays we walked up to Tudor Gardens to collect our aunt and then we'd all walk down to John Street to collect Nan. Next we called at Powell's (later Everett's) the baker to pick up some rolls and then we'd spend the rest of the day on the beach. We did that nearly every day in summer.

Nan came to lunch every Sunday. She would put two dining room chairs outside her house in John Street so that she could be picked up right outside her front door. A lot of Londoners came down to the beach, especially on Sundays, and if she didn't do that the space would be filled up with trippers parking their cars.

Vivien Pask (née Cox)

SIX

Trades and Tradesmen

VILLAGE SHOPS

We had lots of shops in Shoebury High Street, including three butchers, Co-op, World Stores, Barney's hardware and Owen's electrical where we used to go to get the accumulator recharged and carry it home with great care so we didn't spill anything. The chemist, boot mender, haberdashery, hairdresser, Howard's Dairy, Burrows' newsagent, 'Big Parkins' grocers and Everett's bakers. We also had a bank, a hotel, a garage and a doctor's surgery. There was a café on the corner of Smith Street and then Jeff's Café near the station and Fisher's Café, both used a lot by the railwaymen,

There were also a lot of corner shops, including Veseys on the corner of Shoebury Avenue and Wakering Avenue, Humberstone's on the corner of Wakering Avenue and Southchurch Avenue, Miss Beasant's in Friars Street, Miss Bird's further down the High Street, and two in Rampart Street, 'Little Parkins' and Jackson's sweet shop. There were three shops and a café in Smith Street.

J. Tibbles, a baker and confectioner at 22 High Street, on his delivery cart, *c.* 1920. (Peter Owen)

James Glasscock with Jack, *c.* 1900. Glasscock ran an ironmonger's next to the railway station and became a respected member of Shoeburyness Urban District Council. (Angela Burchill and Victoria Currell)

Two of the characters I remember were Mr Wright, the chimney sweep who lived in the High Street next-door-but-one and trundled his equipment round on a handcart and when he came to sweep our chimney, I had to go outside to see if the brush had appeared at the top. The other one was the local window cleaner, who was very scruffy, bent-up little man called Barney who also trundled his ladders round on a handcart and lived in Gothic Row.

I remember the two Miss Mays who lived at the Pyghtle getting on the bus with arms full of flowers that they grew in their garden and took to the florist in Southend. There was a small hall on the edge of their land facing the road, which was one of the venues where we performed with Mrs House's Merrymakers.

Margaret Hammond (née Newman)

ONLY ONE WINDOW CLEANER

There was only one window cleaner in Shoebury during and after the war. He was Bill Barnes, who lived in Gothic Row. He used to go round Shoebury with his ladder on a wheelbarrow; he was only 5ft tall. Every night he would walk round from Gothic Row to the Shoebury Hotel with his jug and get his two pints of ale, every evening.

Bob Dack

MEMORIES OF GREAT-GRANDFATHER

James Glasscock had a furnishing and ironmongery shop in Shoebury High Street from the late 1800s. The shop did well and James became one of the first car owners in Shoebury. He was a fantastic character with a great sense of humour and my mother, his granddaughter, thought he was lovely. This jolly, friendly man preached Presbyterian services at the garrison, set up Shoebury's first Sunday school and served on Shoeburyness Urban District Council. His wife, Susannah, was a quieter personality; she worked in the shop.

Angela Bowhill (née Brewer)

FREE ICE LOLLIES

There was a little green on the corner of Shoebury Avenue and when the baker came by with his horse-drawn cart, the horse always had to go on the green. All the tradesmen came round with their horses – the coalman for example. These horses, with the Army horses, provided us with manure every day.

One of our favourites was the ice man who came round with a huge block of ice on his cart for delivery to Howard's Dairies in the High Street. The man would get a huge spike and ram it into the ice to break off a lump. He would then get a piece of sacking to carry the ice in, so it didn't freeze his hands. While he was in the shop, we children would jump up on the cart and take the splinters of ice he had left behind – it was a free ice lolly!

Shoebury was full of shops – the Co-op, bakers, butchers, grocers and greengrocers – but they all went when the Army went.

Ivy Atkins (née Davis)

George Johnson, fruiterer, 105-107 High Street, 1905-1925. By 1923, the Johnson family had seven shops in Shoebury, selling everything from fruit and fish to flowers and tailoring. (Gillian Blackall)

Above left: George Johnson around 1924 outside his florist shop at 74 West Road with Dolly, one of his five daughters. Gillian Blackall says, 'When the soldiers came down to the beach to swim, my mother, Rose Johnson, used to run away with their clothes!' (Gillian Blackall)

Above right: George Johnson's fishmonger, 74a West Road, 1923-1925. (Gillian Blackall)

HOT PEASE PUDDING

My sisters and I were enthusiastic customers of Banks and Franks, sweet shops almost opposite the station in the High Street. In the '30s, we youngsters seldom replied, 'Going up the High Street' when asked where we were bound; the usual reply being 'Banks and Franks'.

Where the tramway track crossed the High Street *en route* to the New Ranges would be stationed, at night time anyway, an iron-wheeled wooden caravan-type vehicle. This had a full-width opening flap, via which the occupant would dispense hot pease pudding from a very large enamel basin. He would place a large square of greaseproof paper in the palm of one hand, scoop out a portion of the pudding with an enormous wooden spoon, slap it down into the paper, screw up the four corners and – for the price of 1*d* – hand it over to be eaten, by hand, on the way home. Delicious!

John Perrin

COLD STARCHED COLLARS

I can remember taking my father's collars to a shop in West Road at the corner of Cambridge Road where an old lady would cold starch them for 2*d* and put them in a box for me to bring home. This was probably 1938, before I started school. The shop later became a bakers, Faulkner's.

There was no bus service to Southend. My mother would walk to Southend and back with my brother and myself in the pram, although I don't expect she did this very often.

Mary Major (née Prime)

SUNDAY SHOPPING

There was a sweet shop in Rampart Street that we knew as 'Jacksons', run by two sweet, little old ladies, and I remember the New World Stores in the High Street where sugar was weighed out into blue paper bags.

West Road was a lovely shopping centre; you could buy whatever you wanted there. There was Greenfingers run by two sisters, Self the butcher, Knight's the hardware store, Theedom's for fish and chips, Gamage's, a big haberdashery store, and Parkes the chemist up on the corner of St Andrew's Road. Frank Longstaff ran a sweet shop on the corner for years. There were certain things you were not allowed to buy on a Sunday (for example, washing powder), but if you went into Longstaffs, Frank would wrap it up under the counter so no one could see and sell it to you.

Vivien Pask (née Cox)

CAMBRIDGE TOWN CORNER SHOPS

The 'hub' of the Cambridge Town shops in my youth was at the crossing of St Andrew's Road and West Road. On the south-west corner was Goslings the drapers, the domain of the two Miss Goslings, dressed in typical Victorian style black. Goslings always seemed a huge shop to me when I was a boy and those two formidable ladies somewhat intimidating behind their counter! Next to them in West Road was Hooper's the hairdressers. On the right of the corridor inside were the 'ladies cubicles', the exclusive domain of Mr Hooper Snr and Fred. On the left was the gent's salon, where Jim cut hair and passed on the latest gossip.

Mr Offord with Coote & Warren coal merchants' cart in Rampart Street. (Doreen Penlington)

Coote & Warren coal merchants' delivery cart in West Road, just beyond the junction with Sea View Road. Robin Mann says, 'What a job! All done by hand and all the time working in and covered with black coal dust.' (Doreen Penlington)

On the opposite side of West Road stood the off-licence presided over by Captain Burchill. Across from Burchill's was Appleyard's the chemist, a real old-fashioned chemist, with shelves of patent medicines and pills, and huge glass jars full of mysterious, coloured liquids. Johnny Parkes worked there as a young man before eventually taking the shop over. On the other corner of the crossroads was Apps the tobacconist, confectioner and newsagent.

On the west side of the junction of Sea View Road with West Road was Mason's the greengrocer. The shop window always had a tempting display of fruit and vegetables and inside was a row of open-topped sacks making a short aisle to the counter: potatoes, carrots, parsnips, turnips, onions, together with sacks of greens and cabbage, all unwashed, straight from the farm and all in season.

Next on that side was Adey's the sweet shop – rows of glass jars on shelves full of homemade sweets, boxes of liquorice wheels, sherbet fountains and toffee bars that had to be broken up with special hammers. Mr Adey in his white apron weighing them out into white (not brown) paper bags – sugar almonds, jellies, humbugs… wonderful!

Mr and Mrs Scholls had a sweet shop on the other side of West Road but sold proprietary, not homemade, sweets and fizzy drinks like lemonade and ginger beer. Their particular speciality was homemade custard ice cream, which was always a treat. Opposite Scholls was the double-fronted Whent & Belton, facing Sea View Road.

Walking down West Road to the corner of Cambridge Road (now Avon Way) one came to Barney's the outfitters. This always seemed a warm, homely little shop – an offshoot of the larger Barney's in the High Street. Next up the road came Faulkner's the bakers on the opposite corner of Cambridge Road.

Just beyond Grove Road was Dobson's coal yard. Mr Dobson made regular deliveries to our house, with his lovely old horse pulling a cart stacked with various grades of coal. He would carry the sacks one at a time on his back, tipping the contents out over his shoulder into our coal shed.

On the same side as Dobson's yard, on the corner of Waterford Road, stood one of my favourite corner shops, Cramphorns, suppliers of animal and pet food and paraphernalia.

Robin Mann

TEA WITH THE BAKER

There were so many shops in Shoebury High Street at one time, it was unbelievable; four banks, for example. We used to walk the dogs on the beach on a Sunday morning and would call in for sweets from the shop in Rampart Street run by two little old ladies. The milkman would come round with deliveries, of course, and the Co-op baker used to pull his cart round with bread. Mr Bearman the baker always came into our house for a cup of tea with Mum.

Maureen Clark (née Keys)

A TINY MAN ON A THREE-WHEELER

Parkes the chemist in West Road was a cracking bloke. Rather than go to the doctors you could go to Parkes and he'd put you right, although Doctor Ryan and Doctor Dockery were both nice men.

A tiny man on a three-wheeler bike used to deliver from Hannington's, the dairy on the corner of Ness Road and Waterloo Road. I think his name was Bill.

Charlie Hales, the rag-and-bone man, lived in Cambridge Road. He was a great character and very well thought of; a very nice man. He went round with his horse and cart buying any old scraps, but he didn't have a yard, he kept all his stuff in his back garden and he kept his horse over at Freezers.

Keith Bailey

RAG-AND-BONE

Charlie Hales was the rag-and-bone man. He was a real character who lived in Cambridge Town. Sometimes you'd see his horse walking down Campfield Road by itself – it had got away.

Ray Church

LOVELY BEANS ON TOAST

Jeff's Café, opposite the station entrance, served the most wonderful beans on toast – it was lovely!

At Easter when they were selling hot cross buns you had to queue up at Denis the bakers. I'm sure other bakers sold them, but the ones from Denis' on the corner of Ness Road were the best.

Chick's yard was down by Dangers Bridge after the war. There was a pile of scrap metal there piled up as high as the bridge. It was old cars, bits of aeroplane and all sorts of scrap metal; a massive heap.

Joyce Taylor (née Robinson)

A KINDLY MAN

I remember Dr Paddy Ryan as a short, rounded Irishman with rimless glasses who drove large cars and appeared to have to strain his neck to see over the dashboard!

In the mid-1940s, the shop immediately outside the garrison entrance was known to me as the Shoebury Pharmacy and was managed by a Mr Corden. I was a regular visitor to this shop where Mr Corden provided me with much encouragement and practical help in my pursuit of a career in chemistry.

The former Kirby's store in West Road was used as a general grocery store by the Sach family in the 1940s. The family were devout Christians who attended the Peculiar People's Chapel just a few steps to the north of their shop. Mr Sach was a kindly man and a godsend to several Shoebury families who sometimes (or even regularly!) found themselves short of money, because he would extend credit for their essential purchases.

Derek Palmer

MOTHER DIDN'T RECOGNISE ME

Stock's was our sweet shop on the corner of Vincent Crescent, and Mick's Café was popular with young people. I remember Hannington's Dairy in Waterloo Road and Gamidges in West Road. There was Birch the electrical shop where you took your radio accumulator to be re-charged. Shirley from Faulkner's Bakery taught us dancing and we put on shows. For one particular show, I had to wear black with orange spots and I had my hair curled at the hairdressers. When she got to the concert hall, my own mother did not recognise me – she'd never seen me with curly hair!

Doreen Biles (née Scott)

Doreen Biles (*née* Scott) and colleague outside Griffiths, Ness Road, *c.* 1946. Vivienne Odell remembers, 'I only went to Southend once a month; I didn't need to as we had everything here in Shoebury. We bought our tomatoes from the smallholding at Friars Farm and strawberries and tomatoes in Wakering Road.' (Doreen Biles)

Above left: Shoebury High Street, 1934. The building on the far corner of George Street, seen here on the right, is Cook's butchers shop. (Peter Owen)

Above right: Shoebury High Street, 1940s, where customers have parked to use local shops, such as Everett's the bakers. Ann Burtle remembers, 'The smell of the newly baked rolls coming out of the big ovens was wonderful.' (Peter Owen)

COMICS FROM THE SIGNALMAN

There were three grocers shops near our house: Vessy's in Shoebury Avenue, one in Friars Street and one on the corner of Southchurch Avenue. In the High Street was Parkes' electrical shop and Mrs Fisher's café, which a lot of the railmen used for snacks and lunches, later to be Bill Fisher's tackle shop. There was a fish and chip shop and also Legg's the butchers where once a week we used to queue for homemade pease pudding, faggots and saveloys, carried home in a basin wrapped with a cloth to keep it warm.

On Saturday mornings we would walk over the rail footbridge, collect comics from the signalman in his signal box, and then go down the lane to the cinema; everyone called it the Bug Hutch for some reason.

Brian Kane

VENTRIS FAMILY BUILDERS

Between 1880 and the First World War, the Ventris family built the water tower and a great deal of Shoebury High Street. John Ventris, a builder and stonemason, built the Shoeburyness Hotel, including the ornamental facing bricks. He worked with a man called 'Giant' Parkins, who was a tiny little man. Every day, 'Giant' walked to Shoebury from Great Wakering where he lived and where he had been engaged to a lady for fifty years. My grandfather built the Palace Cinema and Auntie Olive played the piano there.

My great-grandfather had built homes at Shoeburyness but then had to demolish them again to make way for the station.

George Ventris

FISH AND CHIPS – A RARE TREAT

I used to go to the shops in Ness Road for my Mum... Pipes the bakers for doughnuts and nelson (a cake made from stale cakes, like a bread pudding, between pastry), fish and chips...2*d* fish and 1*d* chips (although fish and chips were a rare treat!) and milk from Hannington's dairy.

Betty Harrington (née King)

CUSTOMERS KNOWN BY NAME

Shoebury High Street always seemed to be busy and bustling, customers were known by name, births, deaths and ailments all noted and it was the done thing to pass the time of day with people – no wonder it used to take me so long to do my mother's shopping on a Saturday morning!

Outside the gate by the barracks was Mr Corden the chemist (always in his winter coat!) and on the other side of the road was the garage, Jenkins'. Many is the time my bike was taken there to have a puncture mended – that was what a garage was for, very few people had a car in those days. Next to Jenkins' was the Shoebury Hotel and next to that was the café, then the shoemender's. Opposite was Mr Owen the wireless shop, and then Parkins the grocer and greengrocer – one could queue for an hour while things were weighed and put into conical paper bags, made while you waited. Then Barney's the haberdasher and men's clothier with its glass-topped counters and tall stools; then came Everett's (enough said!). Next Ballard's (hardware and shoes); then the barbers and haberdasher's, Gooches, and then Dewhurst's the butchers and the World Stores.

I remember the first day they sold cut bread – everybody shopped at the World Stores to buy this new product. My father [Ted Everett, the baker] was devastated; sales dropped dramatically that week and he had to buy a bread slicer to win trade back again! If I remember rightly, there was then the Co-op butchers and grocers on the corner of George Street. Across the road was Cook's the butchers, then Ham's the haberdasher, the dairy, Godbold's the fish shop, Jeff's Café and Fisher's, the workmen's café. There was also Burrows the newsagent, plus a bank and the doctors, both in houses on the west side of the High Street.

Gloria Burwell (née Everett)

EVERETT'S THE BAKERS

Grandad worked on the railway but Dad, Edward 'Ted' Everett, worked as a Master Baker in the Navy before the war. When he came back to Shoebury he bought Powell's bakery in the High Street and it became Everett's. We lived above the shop, No. 12 High Street, where I enjoyed helping out in the shop and the bakehouse – putting the cream in doughnuts and putting the crosses on the hot cross buns. I had to walk over to the YMCA (now the Garrison Arms) every night and take their order for the next day. Another of my jobs was to sweep the yard every night. At least I didn't have to do the washing – the laundrymen took all the towels and sheets away and brought them back clean the next week.

The bread would be delivered on a trade bike with a big basket on the front and I sometimes accompanied Dad in his three-wheeled, battery-powered bakery van. We'd start in the High Street then deliver to the Bird Cages soldiers' quarters, then go up to Elm Road and Wakering Road. There were about ten cafés in Shoebury, most of them full of soldiers, and Dad supplied them all with bread and cakes.

My father died in 1965 and the bakery was sold to Derek Denis.

Julia Kalogerides (née Everett)

WHENT & BELTON, WEST ROAD

Whent & Belton was a double-fronted shop facing Sea View Road. Through the central entrance door on the left-hand side was a grocery store – butter, cheese, sugar, tea, etc. (much of it to be weighed out from large containers), as well as an array of tinned foods.

On the right was the butchers shop with large meat carcasses hanging from steel rails attached to the rear wall. In front of these, at right angles to the shop front, stood a big, wooden bench, which served both as a counter and a meat chopping block. Between the two stood the large figure of Hubert Belton in his cap and overall coat, usually with a meat cleaver or knife in his hand, and the much smaller figure of 'Wal' Whent in his straw boater and apron weighing out the cuts for the customers. Inspiring figures both of them, but the thing I remember most is the sawdust! There seemed to be sawdust everywhere! You walked in it as soon as you entered the shop, it was always being thrown on and brushed off the bench, and you walked it out of the shop when you left. The Whents were a prominent Shoebury family in those days, and the Beltons farmers on Foulness.

Robin Mann

West Road around 1930, remembered as a wonderful shopping centre. (Peter Owen)

Fred and Emily Cause, respected members of the community, pictured in the garden of 117 High Street, *c.* 1944. As a young man, Fred once broke his thumb trying to ride a pig. In later life he became a respected councillor on both Shoeburyness and Southend District Councils. At home he smoked his pipe while tending his beloved rose garden and conservatory of flowers. Emily, born in Earthpit Cottages and a former parlourmaid at South Shoebury Rectory, was a sweet, old lady adored by everybody, particularly by her husband. They celebrated their Golden wedding anniversary at the Shoeburyness Hotel, which extended its opening hours in their honour. (Caroline Gibb)

A 'DOUGHTY WARRIOR'

My great-grandfather, Fred Cause, was born in 1872, youngest son of an agricultural labourer but he went on to become one of the most influential and respected men in Shoebury.

Great-Grandfather began as a market gardener, renting and later buying land and delivering produce to his customers far and wide. He opened a greengrocers at 40 High Street about 1900 but had to retire from deliveries when the Army commandeered his horses during the war.

In his private and public life, Great-Grandfather was always helping someone sort their problems out. During the Depression, for example, he and Emily opened a soup kitchen to help their fellow villagers. He was volunteer captain of the Fire Brigade and made toys for the Methodist Church bazaar.

He joined the Children's Health Committee and was involved in the Rochford Hospital Board of Guardians, later becoming an active member of the Shoeburyness Urban District Council. He is remembered for standing up for what he believed in, and he remained a councillor when Shoebury was absorbed into Southend in 1933, retiring at the age of eighty-two.

Great-Grandfather's obituary remembers him as a 'doughty warrior'.

Caroline Gibb

SEVEN

Working Life

PARLOUR MAIDS AND FARM GIRLS

One of my mum's first jobs was a parlourmaid in Thorpe Hall Avenue. Her parents lived in Braintree and she only got one half-day a week off and before she was married she used to go home on that half-day.

When they lived at Shoebury, Dad used to go by bicycle to Southend every day where he worked for Southend Corporation, on the London Road. One snowy day he walked and was five minutes late. Wasn't that a long way? He went on his bicycle for thirty-five years, right up until he retired.

My older sisters worked as maids at North Shoebury House. The woman there wanted to adopt my sister Rosie – she told my mum she had enough babies.

My sisters also worked on a farm before the war and at Christmas all the farm girls used to go come see my mum. And my brother used to bring his whole football team home. They'd sit around the table and bang on it for food – how rude!

Iris Lazell (née Wharton)

QUITE A GOOD PAPER ROUND

Before I went to school I delivered papers for Mrs Bates in West Road on my bike. First I'd deliver to South Shoebury Hall Farm. Then I'd go up the lane by the cinema to Grove House, which was a beautiful building similar to RE House that still stands in Ness Road, with a big pond at the front and an air raid shelter at the back.

Further along the lane were two water towers, one built of brick and one built of steel, and then a little bungalow.

Then I delivered to the Army canteen and barrack blocks. I went along Campfield Road to Shoebury High Street, Rampart Street and up to Elm Road; along past the brickfields to Ness Road; then over Danger Bridge to deliver to Bridge Cottages, New Farm and Moat House. Then I'd go to North Shoebury Hall, where a cowman lived. That was an imposing building, with a lot of farm buildings and outbuildings. I went past the Pyghtle, opposite which was a pair of farm cottages and then a block of four cottages. Then I'd go round the back of North Shoebury Post Office and deliver papers to the cottages there.

Then I went back to the White House, a lovely building with a pond. Apart from some cottages on the north side of Bournes Green Road, it was all farmland around there. Then I'd

Gladys Leaney (*née* Cause) in charge of the book department at Boots, late 1920s. (Caroline Gibb)

come down Poynters Lane and up a little path to a bungalow called Croften, which is now a house; past North Shoebury House to two cottages on the corner of Star Lane (now gone) and continued along Poynters Lane.

By the time I got back to Elm Road there would loads of men coming along on their bikes going to work at the AWRE, bikes being the main form of transport then.

So, it was quite a good paper round… then I went to school.

Keith Bailey

NEWSPAPER BOY

I delivered newspapers for Burrows in the '50s. One boy had to get to Southend High School and if the papers were late, because the train was late, we had to do his round for him – at no extra money. That is one reason why I gave up my job there. I also had to deliver to the Officers' Mess in the garrison. In those days, when you applied to work you had to get permission from the Welfare Officer, Mr Tiffin, and there was a card which said you started at seven o'clock in the morning and at five in the evening. But Burrows and that lot, the military, wouldn't have that for evening time. They used to ring up at 4.30 p.m. and say 'Where's our newspapers?' and Mr Burrows would say, 'Well, the boy's gone out'.

When I got to the Officers' Mess, a little dapper boy would come out and say 'What time do you call this?' and I would say, 'You're lucky you got them at quarter to five because I shouldn't start till 5 p.m.' In the end I'd had enough and I gave up. I just chucked it.

Left: Burrows newsagent, Shoebury High Street, where many a Shoebury lad had a paper round. Michael Robinson worked on a milk round; the milkman also played football for Shoebury Town.

Below: The office staff of the Inspection Department, New Ranges, Shoeburyness, photographed at Christmas, 1918. (Tony Hill)

When I moved to the Cambridge side of Shoebury, I worked for Longstaffs and the money was great. If one guy didn't turn up, Ernie Longstaff would say, 'Can you do so and so's round?' and when we came back he'd say, 'Here's your money, half each'. He had a Talbot Sunbeam, a lovely car it was. Well, there weren't many cars around in those days. He was a good man, but he committed suicide.

Roger Bacon

CRICKET SCORES AND WET FISH

As a lad, I used to spend many hours during the cricket season putting up the numbers on the scoreboard alongside the garrison cricket pavilion. This would get me free tea and sandwiches in the interval.

Then, in the football season, it would be over to No.1 football pitch adjoining the cricket ground. This had a good, open-air stand made out of target boards and was the home venue of Shoebury Town. Some of the players' names still come to mind; Codshead Reading, Topper Brown, Lew Keys (the best kicker of a dead ball I have ever seen), Stewy Holt and Shakes Hodges.

From about the age of twelve I worked for Jock Godbold, evenings and Saturday mornings. We did 'wet, dried and fried'. Most fish came down fresh from Grimsby but we used to smoke it ourselves behind the shop; haddock, herrings and bloaters. On Saturday mornings I had to deliver fish and chips wrapped up in newspaper on a trike for up to twenty families and I would get a couple of coppers tip.

I also worked for Ted Everett's bakers, delivering rolls to the garrison NAAFI and the canteen in the New Ranges on a bike with a big box with wheels on the front. I delivered to Brickeen when they had a 'do', like at the bowls club.

I joined the railways as a junior porter at the age of fifteen at Shoebury station and at sixteen I became a fireman on the engines. Soon after I started there was a strike – they were trying to get 8s for the drivers and 5s for the firemen. I didn't go on strike because when I went home and told my mum about it, she said, 'The day your keep money is not on the table is the day your bags is on the doorstep!' So I went back to work. They went back for 8s for the drivers but nothing for the firemen – they just couldn't afford to be on strike any longer.

While I was there I used to collect bets on the station and take them across to the level crossing man, the man with the red flag. He was a runner for the local bookie.

Bob Dack

MESSENGER BOY

One of my first jobs was as a messenger boy for Barney and Ballard the hardware shop. I worked from 8.30 a.m. to 7.00 p.m. on Mondays, Tuesdays and Thursdays, until 1.00 p.m. on Wednesday, until 8.00 p.m. on Fridays, and until anytime he liked on a Saturday – as long as there were customers, he stayed open.

On Wednesdays and Sundays I worked at Jeff's Café on Rampart Terrace, I used to put the deckchairs out and got 10s for it. I only got 12s for all that other work I did at Ballard's.

From age thirteen to sixteen I delivered newspapers in the garrison, which was an absolutely wonderful place to go into. The Officer's Mess was marvellous and Beach House had a lovely walled garden. There were so many papers to deliver at the garrison that I had to go back to the shop and get another lot. I earned 2s from Monday to Saturday and 1s 6d for a Sunday.

During the war I was an ARP messenger boy. There was an air raid one Sunday when enemy aircraft were turned back at Canvey Island and 600 bombs were dropped on us that day. I saw quite a bit of damage done to Friars Street. I went out with the warden and was sent on my bike to the Control Centre, which was over the bridge in Elm Road. The shortest route was through the brickfields and I was there by the gasometers when a dog fight started overhead, right above me with the bullets coming down all around, so I got out of there quick!

Arthur Haslehurst

Left: Ivy Davis, aged twenty in 1939, with the British Legion Cup, won for her work with the Shoeburyness Lifesaving and Ambulance Brigade. Ivy remembers, 'My best friend and I joined the Brigade and went to ARP and first aid classes at the Council chambers [now the police station] before the war. We had a tent on the Shoebury Hall caravan park and used to practise our first aid on the campers. The life savers were the swimmers who practised from Shoebury Beach.' (Ivy Atkins)

Below: Shoebury brickworkers, 1913. Local boys would climb onto the horse-drawn carts for a free ride, while the driver attempted to apply his whip behind him. (Ron Henn)

FLOATING POTATO

At age sixteen I was working for Southend Council at Shoebury Park in Elm Road. One of the jobs was to feed the ducks on the island in the middle of the pond. So there I was one day with a big bucket of mashed potato, rowing out across the lake, when the boat began to sink... I went down with the boat but the mashed potato floated off! Luckily it wasn't too deep and it was the summer. I had to get on my bike and cycle home to get changed.

Terry Fane

BRICKFIELDS IN THE 1920S

Clay dug from the brickfields was loaded onto carts and taken to the washmills behind East Beach. The carts were pulled by little donkeys who all had straw hats on. It was a joy to behold, to see them all trotting along, pulling the carts along narrow gauge lines. They lived in the stables on Elm Road.

After Sunday school in the Methodist Church in the High Street it was a favourite game to try to push each other into the malm banks – that wouldn't have done our Sunday best any good!

We used to go onto the brickfields and watch the men at work, making the bricks with 'butter pats'. We knew everyone and they knew us, so our parents would have soon found out about it if we caused any trouble. As my father was working for the MoD, we were also allowed to go down to Barge Pier and watch the men unload the big guns from barges.

The brickmen were the poorest of the workers; the Ministry of Defence workers were mostly ex-soldiers, but it was the railwaymen who were the wealthy people, because they got overtime pay. When they built new houses in Wakering Avenue it was only the railwaymen who could afford them, but they called it 'starve gut' because they had to starve themselves to be able to pay the mortgage.

There were five landing stages on East Beach for the barges – they would bring chalk over from Kent and take bricks up to London. There was a lot going on; it was very lively in Shoebury. You can still see the wooden stumps that held up these jetties.

Ivy Atkins (née Davis)

FELL IN THE MALM PIT

I remember being taken for a walk along Elm Road when I was four or five [1924/25] seeing rows of men seated in long, low-roofed sheds and wide, leather bands revolving around wheels in the roof apexes and one set in the work benches at which the men were seated.

One grey, freezing morning, a day or two before Christmas, my elder brother and sister and I walked down Blackgate Lane to the beach, after a while climbing up over the sand dunes and heading for home. We came across some sloping banks some 4ft high, enclosing a 15ft-20ft square pond, now frozen over. Of course, we needed no second bidding and soon gained the ice to begin sliding. My brother always maintained that, realising the ice was thin, he shouted a warning, but I did not hear it and went straight through!

Brickworkers on the Elm Road brickfields, 1930s. When it rained, everyone ran to cover the bricks. (Gillian Saggers)

Brickworkers, 1930s.
George Ventris remembers,
'Steel plates were laid down
in the brickfields to make it
easier to push the barrows
along.' (Gillian Saggers)

Fortunately for me, the other two managed to get me out of the glue-like stuff. Clothes stiffening with ice, we set off for home, having to negotiate a log over a frozen stream *en route* which I, shaking uncontrollably, managed to fall off, once more crashing through the ice.

I never did find out what a telling-off my elder siblings were given since I was speedily stripped in front of the outhouse fire, washed and tucked up in bed with several hot water bottles, plied with hot soup and left to thaw out. We were later told that there had been at least one drowning in these malm pits.

In the late '20s or early '30s I remember barges, grounded at low tide, being unloaded by horse and cart of acrid, smoking rubbish from, I believe, the capital. This rubbish, known locally as 'the rough stuff', was piled up at the back of the beach above the high water mark.

John Perrin

BRICK MAKING IN THE 1950s

During the 1950s I worked on the brickfields off Elm Road. The clay was dug during the winter months and put into a washmill which stirred the clay so that all the large particles sank to the bottom. Some mills were horse-driven, others were powered by steam. The liquid clay from the top of the washmill was pumped into the malm banks, huge 'boxes', and was left for the water to evaporate. Ashes from people's fires was mixed into it, then it was shovelled into a hopper and from there to the moulding shed. The rectangular moulds were lined with sand from the local beaches. The finished, soft clay bricks were handled between two paddles (like butter pats) and were laid out on long barrows to dry in the sun. Overnight or in rain they were covered by 'ack-caps', an upturned 'V' of wood covered in tar.

A layer of old bricks was laid out at the bottom of the kiln, with the refuse from the sieved ash spread between them. The new sun-dried bricks were stacked up on top of this with another layer of old bricks around them. Then a fire was set in the bottom.

As they worked shifts, several railwaymen took additional part-time work in the brickfields during the summer months when they needed extra labour, for example to carry bricks and load them onto lorries.

John Askew

A BACKBREAKING JOB

My father worked on the railway, as did my grandfather. I started work in the brickworks in the brickmaking sheds, first as a board spreader, working my way up to barrow loader (a backbreaking job), sand moulder and, finally, an outsider stacking the green bricks onto boards to dry out. This was seasonal work, but some of us were kept on during the winter to sort the bricks from the kilns, a nice warm job.

After this, I worked for builder ROC Robinson and also Pattern the builder. I was also a postman at Shoebury Post Office. Some Saturday mornings I used to go on the beach and dig for lug and rag worms and collect soft back crabs for Bill Fisher's tackle shop in the High Street and collect a bucketful of cockles for Sunday tea. Some of us used to put out lines of baited hooks to catch fish, which were left out when the tide came in and collected when the tide went out. Some we kept for ourselves, the rest were sold to the day trippers.

Brian Kane

Left: Ernie Saggers pictured at his brickmaking job in 1937. Bob Dack recalls, 'Mr Cook was the brickfield foreman, as his dad was before him.' And Margaret Hammond remembers, 'We used to walk from the High Street across the brickfields in Elm Road to get to Shoebury Park (or "the playing fields" as we called it). We'd watch the men making the bricks and then put them on pallets to dry, covered by "ack caps". There was a certain smell about the place when they lit the fire under the kiln to bake the bricks.' (Gillian Saggers)

Below: Shoeburyness railyard with the footbridge over the tracks, where children liked to stand, ending up with soot-blackened faces. Ivy Atkins says, 'The railwaymen were the wealthy people in the village because they got overtime pay.' (Doreen Penlington)

A WHACK WITH A CAPE

Eastwood's brickfield was off Elm Road, with malm banks all in a row off the road and sheds where they made the bricks on the opposite side of the road.

The brickfield was a playground for us. They put wooden covers, known as 'ack–caps', over the bricks to dry them and we boys liked to hurdle over them… but your foot went through every other one! Sometimes Mr Kirby or Froggy Howard caught us. If Sergeant Bates caught you, you'd get a whack with his rolled up cape.

There was a watery ditch over there, alive with newts and frogs, which we used to catch. When we were a bit older, age eleven or twelve, we'd go there to smoke.

Dennis Smith

A MASSIVE RAILWAY YARD

There was very little unemployment in Shoebury before the war because there was plenty of work on the brickfields, the Ranges and the railway.

Grandfather Everett was the railway foreman. He wore a bowler hat and a big hunter watch and chain. Two of my uncles were engine drivers and I would go and help them clean the engines. There were plenty of them because Shoebury was the main depot for engines. It was lovely: a massive yard full of engines, carriages, etc. They never had a problem with leaves on the line or ice because they had a sandbox behind the wheel and they could open a little trap to let a little sand onto the rail for grip.

As a child I would lay in my bed in Wakering Avenue and hear the engines whistle and the windows rattling.

Les Dowie

Shoeburyness
Railway Band.
(Doreen
Penlington)

CLEAN ENGINES AND THE KNAPPING FAMILY

The railway was a very big and important employer. 'Buster' Everett was the shed master at the station. He would go in even when it was his day off to see how it was all going on. He took a tremendous pride in the railway, and was a bit of a martinet about getting the engines clean.

My Uncle John worked on the railway with William 'Bill' Cooper, a colour-blind fitter who got a job with Dale Knapping (the last Lord of the Manor) as a coachman and came over to Shoebury by barge. However, Bill Cooper's first job had been to collect Dale Knapping's coffin at Southend Station and bring it back to Shoebury, as the railway didn't come as far as Shoebury then.

Dale's daughters, the Misses Knapping, lived in Blackheath. When they came to visit Shoebury they stayed with Bill and Emmy Cooper at the Red House. Despite their wealth, the Knapping sisters looked as if they hadn't two pennies to rub together. My grandfather did their work in Shoebury as their contractor while George Bracey (I always remember his leather leggings) collected the rents for them. The later rent collector, Mrs Lane, lived in Wakering Avenue with the only garden with railings around it. She was very strict and didn't like to see anyone digging their garden on a Sunday. The Misses Knapping left their money to the Tate Gallery.

George Ventris

PIE FOR UNCLE TOM

Brother Jim and I once or twice shared the adventure of an evening trek from the station along the raised, wooden walkways between the lines of the sidings, dwarfed by the slumbering, hissing giants of the locomotives, nervously feeling their heat as we hurried past to take Uncle Tom, employed there as a shunter, his enamel jug of tea and a warm pie in a neatly-knotted white cloth.

John Perrin

BARGEE

Our grandad, William 'Bill' Ward, worked on the barges for Eastwood's, the brick company. He would be away from home for days at a time, sailing up the coast to Suffolk and beyond, delivering bricks. When our mum was a girl she would go on the barge with him during the summer holidays and get spoilt with sweets from the other bargemen.

When he retired from the barges, Grandad found work cleaning and maintaining the lifeboat at the end of Southend Pier. Despite this and working on the barges all his life, he never learnt to swim – he couldn't swim a stroke.

Someone told us how barges, years ago, would travel up the River Shoe, through what is now Gunners Park, up as far as Caulfield Road.

Vivien Pask (née Cox)

Left: John Scott in his Silvertown Band uniform at 31 Waterloo Road. During the Second World War, John worked as a fitter's mate on the railways and in 1941 received a letter of thanks from the LMS Railway Company for 'the commendable manner in which you acted in extinguishing incendiary bombs dropped in the vicinity of Shoeburyness during a period of enemy activity on the night of June 5th.' Eileen Whalley (*née* Scott) says, 'Band practice was every Sunday morning in a hall in Rampart Street. The band played at fêtes, carnivals and competitions; they even played at Crystal Palace.' (Doreen Biles)

Below: Shoebury Fire Brigade, 1939. (Caroline Gibb)

COASTGUARD OFFICER

When I retired from engineering, I worked at the end of the pier for a while and then became a sector officer of the coastguard at Shoebury. There were four watches a day, changing at one o'clock and seven o'clock. After three months' training I was left on my first solo watch; it was a rough and windy day, so I kept a close eye out. Then I saw a craft approaching Shoebury from Southend Pier. We had some fantastic binoculars that had come from a German submarine, but I still wasn't sure what I was seeing.

I phoned through to the lifeboat station. 'I can see a Viking ship,' I said. 'Yes, I know,' said Bob Chalk, the lifeboat bosun.

It was a replica Viking ship making a round-the-world voyage. However, rough sea in the estuary was proving hard going and I could see the crew were furiously bailing out. They would never have made it to the North Sea so I called out the lifeboat and had them towed in. We pulled the Viking ship up onto the beach with the landing stage winches by Uncle Tom's Cabin, ordered fish and chips for the crew and let them bed down for the night in the coastguard station.

Les Dowie

EIGHT

The Military Presence

A SOLDIER'S SON

My father, Alfred 'Chick' Henn, was a sergeant in the barracks. The stables for the Mounted Section were to the left of the main barracks gate and there were eighteen horses in each stable in the charge of eight men and one sergeant. Dad was in charge of a team of horses that pulled wagons which picked up used armaments from the mud at low tide and I sometimes helped to polish the horses' harnesses and groom the horses.

In the summer, Mr Millbank used the garrison horses and the soldiers to help bring in the harvest. They had plenty of time as there was not much work on range recovery.

As children in the barracks we played a game where the soldiers would draw a circle on the ground near a wall and put coins in the circle. We would then have to bounce a ball against the wall and try to knock the coins out of the circle. Any we knocked out, we could keep.

Above left: Alfred 'Chick' Henn, a sergeant in the mounted section of the Royal Artillery, based at Shoebury. This photograph was taken around 1931 when Alfred was twenty-one. His son, Ron, remembers, 'Dad took part in the tattoos held at the garrison and once dressed up as a Red Indian, for which Mum covered him in cocoa. He had khaki drill trousers, a khaki jacket with a fringe and a headdress made of seagull feathers.' (Ron Henn)

Above right: Experimental Establishment 'Tug of War' winners, 1933. (Robert Dack)

Beyond the stables, towards the sea, was a pair of semi-detached wooden cottages where we lived, with the Hardstaff family as our neighbours. We never needed to come out of the barracks, only to visit the shops just outside the gate.

Ron Henn

REPAIRING THE ARMY BOOTS

I was born in the Military Family Hospital, which is now the Garrison Arms pub. My dad was in the Royal Artillery, stationed at Shoebury barracks. He ran the shoemaker's shop and before I was old enough for school, I used to sit on the bench with the Army boots being repaired. At other times before I started school, I would sit at the back of the Baptist Church with a colouring book while my mother was at the Mothers' Union.

Betty Harrington (née King)

MILITARY ENCOUNTERS

In early childhood at Shoebury I sometimes heard frightening explosions but, beyond 'It's the guns', I never understood their significance. One particular occurrence is indelibly etched in my memory, probably in the pre-Christmas period of 1924 or '25. I'll never know what awoke me but the room was suddenly lit up by a brilliant flash, immediately followed by a single, thunderous 'BANG!' It was a frightening experience.

View from East Beach across the fence to the War Department beach. Out at sea can be seen *Forth* and *Arctic*, the two barges used to hold targets for firing practice. (Peter Owen)

The boundaries of the War Department land were delineated by dull, red ochre-coloured 7ft fences of metal palings and Granny's house, only half to three-quarters of a mile from the experimental range, shook to the thunder of the guns.

Occasionally, the soldiers rode in columns out of the barracks, along the High Street and on into Wakering Road, exercising their teams of horses drawing the smart, gleaming gun carriages. I well remember, on hearing the clop of hooves and jingle of harnesses, rushing out to perch on the lower rail of the five-barred front gate of Grandma's house to watch the cavalcade pass by. Army regulations might sometimes have been bent when one of the riders would respond to our waves with a brief smile and a nod, much to our delight.

Less delightful for a small child, but no less memorable, was the meeting with a burly soldier clumping towards me on the pavement, I on my way to the shops, he on his way to the New Ranges. The soldier, heightened by his uniform peak cap, dwarfed me as he approached in his brass-buttoned dark-blue tunic and white trousers tucked into heavy, knee-high, black leather boots, which creaked and clumped most intimidatingly as he strode purposefully past towards Blackgate Lane and the Ranges.

John Perrin

BETTER THAN FIREWORKS

When the military did night firing, notices were put up telling everyone to open their windows so they didn't get broken. Everyone assembled on East Beach to watch – hundreds of people went out. Searchlights were trained on the target boards, which were on runners with a ship at either end. They used star shells to illuminate the whole area – it was better than Fireworks Night!

Arthur Haslehurst

SHOOT BETWEEN THE BOATS

The Royal Artillery wore white overalls when they went out to recover shells from the sands, so they could be seen. It used to take 100 firings to test one shell, but they tell me that now it only takes one firing.

They also did night firings and I went down with my father to watch. They had boats like Noah's Arks spaced out off the headland, which they used for target practice. The aim was to shoot between the boats, not at them.

People who bought nice properties near New Ranges have had all sorts of funny things driving by their homes, for example aircraft escorted by police. Things often got stuck on the bend of the road and what little traffic there was would have to wait until it moved on again; huge things they were. Once, we saw an aeroplane coming by and it crashed into the door of Red House.

Ivy Atkins (née Davis)

Experimental Establishment runners, May 1930. Tom Mayhew recalls, 'There seemed to be a hierarchy among sportsmen in the Army. If you were a visiting rugby player you were entertained in the Officers' Mess; if you played soccer you were entertained in the Sergeants' Mess; if you were a runner or something like that, I expect you just got a cup of tea!' (Joyce Taylor)

TALKED IN HIS SLEEP

One evening, we children were all supposed to be in bed when we heard a voice coming up the stairs, 'You lot be quiet and get to bed!' It was Frankie Howerd, then stationed at the garrison, who had come round to visit my dad.

Another of Dad's mates, Toddy Lightfoot he was called, told his wife that in the Army you didn't get paid when it rained. That's how he got to keep some of the money for himself. One day he wasn't well and someone came round to their house with his pay. 'That's not right,' said his wife. 'It rained last week.' 'What are you talking about?' said the man. 'You get paid every day in the Army.' The cat was out of the bag!

After the war, Dad worked for the AWRE on the New Ranges, Foulness. He used to lay concrete roads and then the scientists would come along and blow them up. Then he would build something else for them to blow up. He had had to sign the Official Secrets Act so he wouldn't tell my mum anything about what he was working on, but he talked in his sleep, so she always found out anyway.

They would test guns by firing out over the mud flats and Dad was involved in going out to recover the missiles. Once a man sank into the mud. They managed to pull the man out, but not his boots – they were left behind stuck in the mud!

Bob Dack

TWO TELEPHONE EXCHANGES

In 1938 my dad became a telephone operator for the Royal Corps of Signals at Shoebury, where the telephone exchange was in the barracks clock tower. His uniform was riding breeches and a long tunic with a dog collar and he served throughout the war.

After the war, Dad was demobbed but carried on at Shoebury as a civilian. There were two telephone exchanges by then, one at Horseshoe Barracks and one on the New Ranges. When he was on duty, Dad wore a blue and white armband, which gave him access to various areas. He enjoyed the work as the telephone exchange was in the heart of everything going on. There were half a dozen staff working there, who were a close-knit group working in a very congenial atmosphere.

Tom Mayhew

A RAMPANT ENGINE

As a National Serviceman in the late 1940s, I found out that there were three different ways of getting to the Ranges from the barracks: by walking, by lorry or, surprisingly, by military train. In fact, one of the first things I recall about the Ranges was the railway system which seemed to branch out in all directions; we soon learnt to keep sharp look out when crossing the rails to avoid being run down by anything from a rampant engine to a railway-mounted, self-propelled NAAFI wagon.

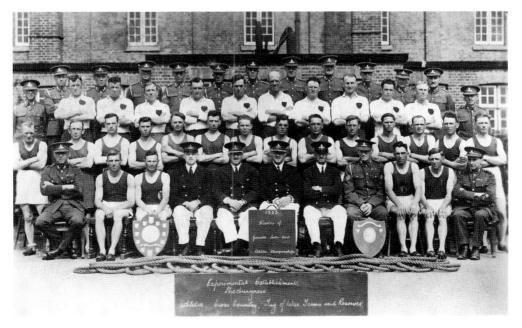

Winners of the Garrison Inter-unit Athletic Championships, 1933: the Experimental Establishment Athletic, Cross Country and Tug of War teams. (Joyce Taylor)

One of our static radar sites, B3, was just a little wooden hut with an aerial attached to the roof, rather out in the wilds. It was the task of the radar operator to time the flight of shells by starting a stopwatch at the sound of the gun, picking up the shell blip on the radar screen and stopping the watch when it disappeared. It was not a difficult task but required a fair degree of concentration. If firing went on all day it could get rather tiring on the eyes – not to mention the overworked stopwatch thumb! Once, after a long day, I realised that, by oversight, nobody had been detailed to pick me up, so I hitched a lift on a RHA horse and wagon. By the time we had ambled back to barracks, the canteen and NAAFI were closed and all the lads from my billet had gone out for the evening. There was nothing for it but to go round to that little late night café near the Shoebury cinema – a haven for tired, fed up and starving gunners.

John Wenning

GYMKHANAS AND TATTOOS

One of my earliest memories is hearing soldiers running past up the High Street and Wakering Road on their training exercises. You'd see the horses with their gun carriages too, trundling up the High Street for exercise.

The horses took part in gymkhanas and tattoos held in the New Ranges as entertainment for the villagers of Shoebury. They'd have races with the gun carriages; it was really exciting for children. The men would be wearing little black hats and blue uniforms.

Maureen Andrews (née Rawlings)

A GALLOPING MAJOR

The soldiers and the railway were the mainstay of the town. The barracks was huge with loads and loads of soldiers. One major used to gallop down the High Street on his horse to preach at the New Ranges and then back up again to preach at the garrison church. We knew him as 'the galloping major'.

Joy Bateman (née Gilbey)

HORSES AND BICYCLES

The garrison horses, six or eight pulling a gun carriage, went up and down the High Street four times a day. We kept a bucket and shovel just inside our front gate and when the horses had gone by, we had orders to go out and collect what they had left behind. If it was nearer our house, it was ours, but if it was nearer to our friend June's house, that was hers. If it was in the middle we used to go and have a fight for it! Dad would put it in a bucket of water and water the tomatoes with it.

Experimental Establishment winners of the Inter-unit Athletics 1935: Tug of War, Football Cup, Billiards and Darts. Margaret Chaplin says, 'The garrison was very involved with Hinguar Street School. School sports day was held over there, for example.' (Joyce Taylor)

One of the few times we were allowed in the garrison was for the public tattoos, which were a show of what they could do. They had tanks on display and soldiers wearing tight tunics with yellow braid and buttons and a feather on their hats, riding horses. I remember the helicopters swooping down to make a display with coloured smoke, and one year the Gurkhas took part. The gymkhana and Army sports day were other big events.

The Army men who worked on the Experimental Ranges, the XPs, wore a white uniform with black boots, khaki gaiters and a black peak cap. As well as them you had the 'checkies', the civilian workers. Some of them worked with the horses picking up shells from the mud after they'd been fired. The horses came along the High Street at four o'clock, going back to the garrison with six horses to each of five or six gun carriages. Then the checkies would leave work at five o'clock and they'd come along Blackgate Road three or four abreast on their bikes, a great rush of people; the road was filled with bikes. There was also a little single-decker bus painted dark green, which worked as a shuttle bus between the New Ranges and the railway station for the workers.

Margaret Chaplin (née Bates)

POLISHING THE HORSES

My brother-in-law, Sergeant Harrison, was in charge of polishing and cleaning the horses in the garrison. They had to look really smart and he loved his job. One really cold winter when it was all iced over, they put sacks on the horses hooves and one horse slipped over.

June Edwards

The garrison water tower, pictured from the lane behind the Palace Theatre.

SCRUMPING FOR APPLES

We used to go in the garrison quite a lot to play – mainly because we weren't allowed to! With the Grove Road gang we'd go scrumping and get loads of apples and pears from the fruit trees behind the single officers' quarters on Warrior Square Road. One time, the War Department police saw us; we tried to run off and chucked the apples away but they chased us and caught us. They took us to the guardroom and kept us in there for a while to frighten us, then let us go.

Down on the firing range there was a big mound with targets in front of it, where they used to practice. We'd pick up lead from the spent bullets and take it to Chick's scrapyard (where Watson Close is now) for money.

There were underground gun emplacements on the garrison too, up by the coastguards. We called it 'the maze'. You'd get in down some steps that led to lots of passages with different rooms coming off them. The rooms had slits in for shooting out of. There were two or three entrances, and it must have covered quite a large area.

Keith Bailey

THE ORIGINAL BATWOMAN

My youngest boy wasn't at school yet when I wanted a little job so I took a batwoman's job, 9 a.m.–12 p.m. in the garrison. I worked for the wife of Major Lyons in the Terrace quarters, where the cricket ground is; blooming great houses they were. So I did the housework while the wife ran a nursery for twelve children. Then I would go and perhaps help out with the youngsters. But before that we never went into the garrison; we weren't allowed to.

Betty Harp (née Bates)

ST WINIFRED WINKED

The Padre of the garrison church was from Northern Ireland. He liked to tell us children about the stained-glass windows. There is one of St Peter cutting off the ear of the High Priest and the ear is there in the window. There is also St Winifred who, the Padre said, used to wink at us.

After the war, most of the soldiers went away apart from a 'holding group' at the garrison. Every Good Friday the local churches held a combined service in the garrison church and I was the last organist there. The organist before me was a blind man but he had started to get a bit confused and would stop in the middle of a hymn, so they had to let him go. They had services at the garrison church for weddings, funerals, Armistice Day, the Sunset Ceremony, Normandy veterans' reunion, the British Legion and the Maritime Regiment. The last service held there was on a Christmas Eve; it was so sad. It was a very smart barracks in the good days.

Ivy Atkins (née *Davis*)

A GARRISON CHILDHOOD

We moved to Shoebury barracks in 1951. We used to come and go through the West Gate – there were no actual gates there then, just a guard checking you. At 5 Hilly Marsh, we had a massive garden where Dad kept chickens and Mr Cox next-door-but-one, he kept chickens too. I made a little coop and kept pigeons.

Garrison Church Choir, *c.* 1905. From left to right, back row: Ernest Wright, Samuel Payne, Thomas Wright, Norman Smith, Lewis Busbridge, Frederick Andrews, Albert Richardson, Albert Collins, Vivan Parslow, George Preece. Middle: William Little, Tyson, Turner, an officer, Revd Johstone, Dawson, Clempson, ?. Sitting: Frederick Wright, Jarratt Leaney, Charles Turner, William Dawson, Thomas Parslow, Mick Richardson, Frederick Ketteridge, George Mears. (Caroline Gibb)

The Garrison Choir,
c. 1944. Ron Henn is
pictured at the front
right of the procession.
(Ron Henn)

On the front there was the sergeants' beach and then there was the officers' beach and then there was the squaddies' beach at the East Beach end, with the diving board. I used to swim from the sergeants' beach up to the squaddies' to do some diving, then I'd swim back. Of course, sometimes the tide was against me by then, so I had to swim in and walk back. Then there was a rule come out: no sergeants' children to go on the officers' beach. I said, 'What am I supposed to do then? Do I just stop swimming and drown?' I hated the class distinction but that was the forces for you.

There was a little pier where it was very dangerous and there were several squaddies drowned off there. So you didn't go swimming there. We used to play amongst the gun towers, where all the tanks were.

The firing ranges were between Barge Pier and where the coastguard is now. There was all tunnels under there where we used to play and have fun. In the winter we'd go in there and play tag and light fires.

The tower blocks, we used to go up there and then we'd see the bluebottles (that's what we called the War Department police) coming along. They'd look up but we'd escape down this big electric cable that was cleated right down; we'd scale back down; it was about a 40ft drop. Then down to the sea wall, run along the sea wall to the sergeants' beach and back up the steps and from there we'd watch them looking to see where we were, but we were well away!

We used to walk along the beach but when they were firing on the ranges we'd walk along the sea wall, but keep our heads down. We were only young. In the winter, when it snowed, on the way to Scout group or youth club we'd creep up to the soldiers' billets, open the door quietly, switch the lights off, let them have it with our snowballs and run like hell!! My father would know about it by the next day but they couldn't prove it was us.

And the fires… lighting fires was completely taboo. We used to dig out holes and make a shelter with grass over the top, and just step down and go in, like we'd made a little earth bunker. Then we would light a little fire but make sure there was no smoke coming.

We were always messing about. It was great. Great for children; you had your freedom but you felt safe.

Roger Bacon

OLD RANGES DRAUGHTSMAN

My father and I worked together for a while in the drawing office in Old Ranges with many good old characters. The Chief Clerk was Rod Murray whose daughter Barbara was Southend's Carnival Queen in 1950; she had been at school with me.

One of the first tasks I was given in the drawing office was to visit the officers' quarters opposite the garrison cricket ground adjacent to our office and take measurements in preparation for alterations. The door was opened by the officer's wife. There was a large reception area and a central staircase and standing in the middle of the staircase was a young lady without a stitch on. 'That's my daughter,' said the officer's wife. 'Don't take any notice.' Don't take any notice! To a boy of seventeen!

I thought I was going to enjoy my work, but I didn't really as many of the officers' houses were really awful, very badly kept.

Dave Evans

Jack Emberson (far right) with colleague government workers pictured out on the Ranges. (Gillian Saggers)

A REAL BARRACK TOWN

Shoebury was a real barrack town, full of soldiers and their families. I was lucky enough to go to the riding school in the garrison. Most of the girls were soldiers' daughters but Dad did the bread round in there so I was allowed to go too. I think it cost 1s 6d for a morning's ride. The soldiers took us out on the mud on these big Army horses but we were only ten years old so sometimes the horses would run away with us!

Two girls, daughters of one of the majors, had Shetland ponies called Toffee and Taffee, which I used to love looking after.

I enjoyed the pantomimes, which were held in the big hall just inside the garrison gate, and I also went Scottish dancing there. My grandma used to go to whist drives there and my sister was in the garrison church choir. Dances and children's Christmas parties were held in the soldiers' gym off Campfield Road.

My best friend lived in Beach House. It was a beautiful house with a huge great kitchen. It still had the bells in the kitchen to summon the batman, although the family didn't have one then. The house had squash and tennis courts behind it and, at the front, steps down to the beach.

I had other friends who lived in the majors' houses where I remember the huge, green baize doors. The houses were three-storeys high with high ceilings and huge windows.

Julia Kalogerides (née Everett)

EXTREMELY COLD INDOORS

When 37 Regiment moved to Shoebury in early 1967, my family were quartered in the Terrace. There was plenty of room there and the top floor, the original servants' quarters, was marvellous for the children. We set up the Scalextric track up there, for example. The house had one radiator in the hall, as did all the other Terrace quarters. However, we were lucky to have a radiator on the landing as well. Apparently, a colonel had been in the house before us and he had insisted on a second radiator – but it was still extremely cold in winter with the big, sash windows with no double-glazing.

In December 1979 I began researching the history of Shoeburyness Garrison and my office gradually filled up with artefacts that I either acquired myself or were donated to the collection. Eventually, the growing archive was relocated to the old Barrack Hospital. At first I shared the building with the dental centre and the Housing Office but they later moved out and it was thought unnecessary to refill the oil tank for the heating, so that too became a very cold building. In fact, on occasions, it was colder inside than out and you had to go outside to warm yourself up!

Tony Hill

A LUCKY RESCUE!

I was at my club one night in the 1980s chatting to a friend called John. He said, 'I've got a big job tomorrow, I've got to knock down the Terrace in the garrison.'

The Shoeburyness British Legion outside their headquarters by the railway station. Betty Harp remembers Boundary Day as quite an event, when you could not go on any Army land. (Gillian Saggers)

I said, 'You can't do that, it's Listed! If you knock it down, they'll only make you build it up again.'

So, he waited until the garrison Clerk of Works arrived the next day. The Clerk said, 'Why aren't you at work? Get this knocked down!'

John said, 'I'm not going to knock that down if it's Listed because I'll only have to build it up again exactly the same. Didn't you know it was Listed?'

The Clerk said, 'Yes I did know it was Listed but I didn't think you knew. Now you'd better get off the site!'

Arthur Haslehurst

PAPER ROUNDS AND CURRY NIGHTS

There were hundreds of soldiers around. Their horses would go down the High Street and we'd follow them and get the manure for our gardens or, in our case, for our dad's allotment behind the High Street. If the horse stopped outside your house, then that was yours. You couldn't poach anyone else's manure! The horses came past two, three, six times a day, travelling from the garrison to the ranges and sometimes pulling carts.

The Shoeburyness British Legion darts team, 1939. (Ray Church)

I did a paper round in the garrison, twice a day during the week and once on Sundays. I got 5s in the morning, 4s in the afternoon and 2s 6d on a Sunday, delivering to the billets and the cookhouse. We did all right there because the squaddies got to know us and gave us titbits from the cookhouse. Sometimes we'd get an invitation from the soldiers to go in the Sergeants' Mess, which I loved. David Ascroft, who later became a councillor, was a soldier and invited us to dances there. In the 1950s and '60s they used to have great curry nights in the Sergeants' Mess.

Ray Church

HORSES THUNDERED UP AND DOWN

We married in the garrison church where the Padre was very strict and Mum belonged to the garrison church guild. I enjoyed the Remembrance Sunday services when the troops would all line up and march to the church.

Heavy Army vehicles were always going up and down the High Street and horses from the garrison thundered up and down, collecting stores from the station. The stables were on the left-hand side of the garrison main gate and there were more opposite the clock tower.

Butlins wanted to buy the garrison when the Army left but they couldn't.

Vivienne Odell (née Edwards)

NINE

The War Years

DON'T LOOK BACK

On 2 June 1940, my sisters Joyce and Sheila and me were given a lunch bag, a small case of belongings and our gas masks in a box over our shoulder. With the other children from Hinguar Street School, we were lined up and told to march single file and not look back.

We were put onto coaches and were taken to Southend Central Station where the roads were already lined with buses of children. At our destination in Derbyshire, eighteen of us were taken in by Hollowford Youth Hostel in Castleton, where we spent four happy years under the care of Mrs Rowlands and her family.

During our time away, Mum would organise a coach for the mothers to come to visit us every six weeks or so. The coach was hired from Mr Vickery at Bridge Garages, who, incidentally, ran the first bus service from Shoebury to Southend.

Maureen Andrews (née Rawlings)

I WISH I WAS GOING!

I was six when war broke out, and one of the first things I remember is the schools being evacuated. Mum and Dad didn't have us evacuated; they said: 'If a bomb's got your name on it, it's got your name on it!'

I went down to the railway station on the day the other children left. They all had their gas mask case on a string across their shoulder and a label on and I remember thinking, 'Oh, I wish I was going!' because they were going on a train – but I didn't know they weren't coming back that night.

After that, the half-dozen children left in Shoebury didn't go to school for two years.

There were great, big, square tank traps in the High Street, about 6ft high, across the pavement and jutting out into the road so tanks couldn't go through; a car could get through, but not tanks. The ones in the High Street were great big ones and elsewhere there were smaller round ones, sort of a cone shape.

I've seen the sky full of German planes and one time when we'd been out and were coming back home, a German plane came down and machine-gunned us.

Our house in the High Street backed onto Wakering Avenue, which received a direct hit one night. We were down in our shelter; bombs were coming down, everything was shaking and dust was coming down. Dad didn't think our house would still be standing in the morning, but it was and, in fact, only suffered a few cracks; not even a window was broken.

We did eventually go back to school during the war. First it was just in the mornings at Brickeen in the High Street. Later we took the bus to school at the Sea View Homes.

Margaret Chaplin (née Bates)

LOOK AFTER BROTHER JIM

The first thing I remember about the war is being evacuated. I had a label tied on to my coat and was told to look after my little brother, Jim, who was nearly four years old. I was just six! There were double-decker buses parked outside our school, Hinguar Street, and all us children got on board. I was upstairs and looked out of the window to see my mother standing with two neighbours of ours, with tears streaming down their faces. We were taken up to Hope in Derbyshire.

We were home by the following summer but I already had a Derbyshire accent. Back home, I went out into our garden and saw the tomatoes that Mum had been growing. It was the first time in my life I'd seen a tomato, so I picked one and ate it and Mum yelled at me – that's what I remember about coming home.

Later, the brickfields, which were closed at the time, were a playground for us kids. We used to climb up the stacks of bricks or play around the malm pits; we had no idea that it might be dangerous.

Some of the eighteen pupils evacuated from Richmond Avenue School who spent four years at the youth hostel in Castleton, Derbyshire. Back at home, Ann Burtle (*née* King) and her friends played leap frog over the tank traps in the fields near George Street. (Maureen Andrews)

Left: Pupils from Hinguar Street School at Bamford, Derbyshire, where they were evacuated. Second from right, back row, is the headmaster, Mr Bowyer. (Doreen Penlington)

Below: Pupils evacuated from Richmond Avenue School on 2 June 1940, pictured here in Ashbourne, Derbyshire, with some Gurkhas. Doreen Biles remembers, 'Miss Bangs went with us and Miss Cable and Miss Leaney.' (Doreen Biles)

A stick of bombs fell sometime in the late 1940s on the railway yard and killed Mr Speller, a railway signalman. Bombs fell in the back gardens of Friars Street and Wakering Avenue and blew out all the doors and windows – the doors ended up out in the road.

John Askew

KNITTING BALACLAVAS

Soon after war broke out, they came round wanting us to take soldiers in – we had loads as lodgers in our house because the barracks was overcrowded. American soldiers were billeted in the house next door to us and all the men were after my sister, Gladys. When we heard that Churchill was coming down to Shoebury, we all went up to the railway station to see him.

When the air raid siren went we used to go under the stairs or in the shelter but it was bitterly cold. Some people had done their shelters up really nice but ours sometimes had water in it and it was really cold.

At school during the war we had to knit balaclava helmets for soldiers, but I wasn't very good at knitting so my friend had to help me. Everyone cheered when I finally got mine finished!

I always had to go to the Methodist Sunday school on a Sunday afternoon. There were a couple of little boys there always messing around. One day one of them sang 'There is a Green Hill Far Away' and he sang it beautifully. Soon after that, he and another boy went over the beach with an Alsatian dog and got under the wire and was blown up. They played 'There is a Green Hill Far Away' at his funeral and all the kids were crying.

My brother was held prisoner of war and when he came home we decorated our house with Union Jacks.

June Edwards

SOLDIERS IN THE HOUSE

There were barricades across Sea View Road during the war and when it was the blackout you had to take a torch out with you.

While my brother Arthur and I were away in Derbyshire, three soldiers were billeted at our house. The rules stated that the soldiers were not allowed in the house during the day – they were only supposed to go there for sleeping, but my mother didn't like to see them just walking around so she invited them in and they all used to sit round playing cards. Later, when I returned from evacuation, we had a soldier with his wife and child living with us until they were moved into quarters in Campfield Road.

Doreen Biles (née Scott)

ANTI-AIRCRAFT GUNS

At the outbreak of the Second World War, most Shoebury children were evacuated to Derbyshire and all the schools closed. For the few of us whose parents chose not to let go, some minimal schooling was provided by 'roving' teachers, who taught small assemblies of children living close-by, just for a few hours and usually in front rooms voluntarily provided by residents. Later, the Council arranged for a small school to be set up in the evacuated Sea View Homes in Ulster Avenue.

In 1939, Caulfield Road ended at its junction with Pentland Avenue, and from here to St Augustine's Avenue in Thorpe Bay was open fields. It was here, near St Augustine's Church, that the military mounted a battery of anti-aircraft guns (about ten or more, on concrete bases). When in action, these guns would frequently make the ground tremor, but were still a comfort to local inhabitants who liked to feel that something was being done to deter enemy raiders overhead!

Shoeburyness Home Guard, from left to right: R. Collins, R. Parsons, R. Lodge, Sgt Saggers, L/Sgt Runt, Bdr Turner, Bdr Benny, L/Bdr A. Mate, Gnr Hayward, Gnr Derrick, Gnr Martin, Gnr Bannister, Gnr Larder. (Gillian Saggers)

Shoeburyness Home Guard. Gillian Saggers says, 'During the war they had 16-inch naval guns pointing down the Thames, which were sometimes manned by the Home Guard.' And June Edwards remembers, 'Dad would come home from work, have a drink and then go straight out on Home Guard duties.' (Gillian Saggers)

In addition, during 1944, the Army mounted a single, rapid-firing Bofors gun alongside the red track which crossed the fields between Caulfield Road and Marcus Avenue, to try to intercept German VI flying bombs which were then flying just above rooftop-height between Caulfield Road and the railway line on their way to London. Unfortunately, these aircraft flew very fast, faster than a Spitfire, and the gunners were not very successful in their mission.

The first recovery of a German magnetic mine from the mudflats off the Ness (November 1939) was a significant event in the Second World War, which made the national press headlines at the time.

Derek Palmer

Above left: Ivy Atkins (*née* Davis), back left, with colleagues in the Shoeburyness Lifesaving and Ambulance Brigade, pictured outside their wartime headquarters the Caulfield Road School, which had just been built and had not yet been used as a school. (Ivy Atkins)

Above right: Ivy Atkins (*née* Davis), pictured in her warden's uniform at the air raid shelter in the garden of her home in Shoebury High Street, has these memories of her days as an air raid warden, aged just twenty: 'Our air raid warden's post was in the High Street but I am a heavy sleeper and slept through the night-time raids. In the morning my father would say, "That was a bad one last night; what a noise!" and I would complain that he had not woken me up. "I'm not sending a girl out in that," he'd reply. When I did go down to do my ARP duties, Father would grumble, "I don't like it, a girl out there with all those men."' (Ivy Atkins)

NO BREAK IN THE NOISE

After the First World War, firings went on to test guns. There was no break in the noise of firing for the people of Shoebury. They used to warn us to open the windows before the firing but, even so, plaster came off the ceilings when they tested the big guns. By the time of the Second World War we were well used to it.

A lot of people moved away during the war and their empty houses were occupied by soldiers because the garrison was overflowing. When I was working in Chatham, I had to have a pass to allow me to come home; nobody was allowed to come into Shoebury who didn't have a good reason to be here.

When a magnetic mine was found on the beach one day, my father met Churchill, who had come down to see it. Of course, that could not be publicised as we couldn't let the Germans know they had been found out. So a fuss was made of Churchill inspecting the 'Dads' Army' and the air raid wardens.

Ivy Atkins (née Davis)

MOTHER'S WAR EFFORT

My mother was an air raid warden, based at the square, brick-built ARP hut in Wakering Road. One Sunday afternoon, 18 August 1940, fifty Heinkel bombers were turned back from North Weald airfield by bad weather, AA guns and the RAF. On their way home, they dropped 200 bombs on the sands off Shoeburyness and thirty-one bombs on Shoebury village itself.

Mum went round helping to dig people out of the rubble of bombed houses, as well as helping the wounded and shell-shocked while the bombs were still falling. Afterwards, she received a letter from a senior ARP officer, thanking her and saying she had 'displayed the highest sense of duty and disregard for personal safety when you rendered assistance to casualties'. Colonel Hickman, the Superintendent of Experiments at Shoebury, wrote of his own admiration and Mum was later awarded the Defence Medal.

By 1944, Mum was working on the New Ranges, hedging and ditching, digging and hauling. Several local mothers worked there doing men's hard work, like navvies. For example, they prepared the ground and laid the foundations for the big tower near the beach.

The Civic Restaurant was set up at Hinguar Street School for these working mothers who came by coach every lunchtime for their meal in the school hall. When we returned from evacuation, Mum stayed on and worked on Foulness in the kitchens.

Maureen Andrews (née Rawlings)

GAS MASKS AND SANDBAGS

Early in the war, some men came round, looked at our house in the High Street and said, 'You can take six' and we had six soldiers billeted on us. Later, gun examiners used to come and stay with us for a few weeks at a time, usually two at once. We also had some railway boys from up north.

We had a gas alert post in our front garden. It was like a flat square on a pole and if it changed colour you had to put your gas mask on. We weren't allowed out of the house without our gas masks with us, and Dad made a gas refuge in one of our rooms by filling all the gaps with stuff like papier mâché.

We had strips of brown paper on the windows and sandbags outside the front door. They had dumped sacks in the street with a lorry load of sand and everyone went out and made their own sandbags. Mum once said I could sweep the front step 'but don't move the sandbags'. Well, I was sweeping and a bit of sand kept coming out of this sack so I pulled it out and a great big spider ran out. I ran off down the path thinking this spider would come after me! I went straight over the gate and scraped my knee and I've been frightened of spiders ever since.

In the war, we knew when an oil tanker had been torpedoed – smoke would go up for weeks in a big, black cloud. We once got hundreds of pencils washed up on the beach, but Dad told us not to pick anything up in case it was German – he thought they might be booby-trapped. Another time, we stood and watched the planes dropping mines and when they found the magnetic mine on East Beach and the man went out to defuse it, we all lined up along the promenade to watch him.

Betty Harp (née Bates)

DOGFIGHTS OVERHEAD

Sometimes when I was supposed to go to school I would go down the beach instead and be under one of the upturned boats. During the war, if the siren went when you were on the way to school you were taught to run back home or to the shelters at school, depending on which was nearest – funnily enough, I was always nearer home! The shelters at school were brick-built and had seats all down the side; they smelt of concrete.

When there were dogfights or Spitfires and German planes coming over, we used to go outside to watch. My dad was in the Home Guard. He had a Bren gun and was on the roof of our shed one day firing at the enemy planes coming over while I was standing next to him, watching. An enemy aircraft saw him and came down to shoot; bullets were hitting the ground around me. Then Dad saw me and threw me into the dugout. Another time I saw a house falling down in Wakering Avenue; the wall fell off with the bath still attached to it.

David Odell

NEW RANGES WEATHERMAN

I arrived in Shoebury in September 1939, aged eighteen, to start my new job as a technical assistant in the meteorological office at the New Ranges.

Our job was to transmit hourly weather observations to the Air Ministry. As readings were required twenty-four hours a day, we worked in shifts. Night duty was improved by the opportunity to chat to the young lady in charge of the Shoebury telephone exchange, whose role was to connect us with the Ministry.

Above left: New Ranges Central Office and conning tower. Peter Brewer remembers: 'Wind speeds were recorded by an anemometer in the top cabin of the conning tower. The chart on which the recordings were made had to be changed once a week, which entailed some poor soul climbing up the tower to change it manually. In the winter months this was very cold and, bearing in mind the metal ladders, probably quite dangerous.' (Peter Brewer)

Above right: Churchill inspecting the XP Home Guard, June 1941. Peter Brewer says: 'The Royal Engineers made a makeshift armoured train with two-inch bore Bofurs guns on which we had to do duty. It was fun travelling up the track to Havengore Island and firing shells at a stranded barge out on the shore, sometimes staying out on it all night.' (Gillian Saggers)

Churchill at the
Experimental
Establishment, June 1941.
Peter Brewer, watching
from the window, recalls,
'Someone shouted
"Three cheers for
Winnie!" and Churchill
waved his hat.'
(Joyce Taylor)

The measurements we made were of the wind speed and direction at various heights, which were required for the testing of guns and for the AA batteries. To take the recordings we sent up inflated hydrogen balloons from the roof of the main office, taking readings of their height with a theodolite every minute. For night-time readings, a Chinese lantern containing a lighted candle was suspended from a length of cotton tied to the balloon. We could follow the candle and take readings for half an hour or more. Occasionally, however, we found we'd lost track of the candle and had been trying to take readings from a star!

Later, I transferred to a nine-to-five job under Mr Hemans, the civilian officer in charge. His project was entitled 'The variation of wind with time'. I also assisted Mr Lupton in exploring the effects of weight and wind on the trajectory of shells. Anti-aircraft teams used this information to apply deviation to shells.

A very cold job was to take triangulation readings from the outdoor theodolite stations on the New Ranges. We had to go out in all weathers on our bicycles in our balaclavas; it was very, very cold out there on the sea wall.

In 1942 they brought in women to work as typists, and that's how I met my future wife. All-in-all I have very happy memories of Shoeburyness.

Peter Brewer

SO EXCITING!

In September 1940 the sky was full of German aircraft. It was a wonderful time – no school for a start! We collected shrapnel and when an aircraft was shot down over Lifstan Way we went and got bits of the aircraft. It was so exciting, it was wonderful! I saw a doodlebug over the roof of our cottages once, and I used to stand out there and watch the dog fights. Brilliant!

June 1941, Winston Churchill and Lord Beaverbrook examine a mounted Spandau machine gun recovered from an enemy aircraft brought down locally. Margaret Hammond says, 'When Churchill came we all lined the streets to see him.' (Margaret Hammond)

Of course, having soldiers in the town was nothing new to us. You could hear the bugle call from the garrison all across the town, and I worked as a messenger boy for the ARP, from their post in Ness Road.

Alan Cundy

NO ROOM IN THE SHELTER!

During the war, troops were billeted in the Shoebury Gospel Hall next door to us in Wakering Avenue. When the siren went we sometimes couldn't get into our Anderson shelter because the soldiers had jumped over the fence and filled it up!

During the time the family was evacuated to Bamford, Derbyshire, Dad stayed at home along with the dog, which chewed everything. It got out of its kennel in the garden and got into the hall next door where it chewed all the boots and brushes of the troops billeted there.

I was at Hinguar Street School while the air raids were still going on and we had to get under the desks during the raids. It was a nice school, which always seemed enormous but now looks tiny.

Doreen Penlington (née Gilbey)

GOT ANYTHING TO EAT?

During the war, soldiers were billeted in Richmond Avenue School and the Sunshine Home. Then the government took over private houses for billets as so many were left empty and there was no room in the garrison. In the mornings we'd see the soldiers come out of the houses in Thorpedene Gardens and form up in ranks. Every tenth house or so was a cookhouse and after the soldiers had marched off to the barracks, we kids would knock on the door and ask 'Got anything to eat?' The cook would get a slab of fruit cake out of the cupboard, a big 14lb slab, and say, 'How many of you?' 'Four.' So he would cut off four pieces and we would eat it on the way to school.

In the lead up to D-Day there were military vehicles all down Campfield, Ness Road and along the front, all parked up one behind the other. After D-Day, prisoners of war were brought in. The Italians came first, wearing a yellow diamond on their greatcoats. They were not allowed to use public transport and in the winter the bus would go past them walking to Southend in the driving snow with their greatcoats pulled up around their ears.

My Dad ran the RE stores in the Old Ranges. One day a lorry turned up with six Italian prisoners of war in it and Dad was told, 'These men will be working under you.' One of them became a good friend of the family and kept in touch after the war.

Tom Ambridge

UNCLE ERNIE FOUND A MINE

At the beginning of the war, German planes came right over Shoebury and dropped magnetic mines. They were supposed to sink but one landed on the mud flats and my uncle, Ernie Church, found it while he was out there setting his hooks for fishing. It was the first one they had ever seen.

During wartime we used to go all over North Shoebury collecting rabbit food for our rabbits. Over at Bunkers were three sandpits full of water; we'd make rafts and go out on them, but half of them would sink.

Ray Church

A ROOM WITH A VIEW

Our top floor meteorological office faced the sea and was quite central to the activity on the New Ranges. It could be quite noisy at times, such as when they fired point blank at armour plate, although they did try to warn us of impending loud noises by banging a rail just before it happened.

I was in the office the day Churchill visited the New Ranges in June 1941, and we all watched him from the windows. The 'checkies' (the government workers, so called because they had to check in for their shift) lined up along the road and Churchill walked along the ranks. It was dead silent, with a tenseness in the air. Suddenly someone shouted 'Three cheers for Winnie!' and Churchill's whole demeanour changed instantly and he waved his hat.

We witnessed the Maunsell forts being towed out to their position in the estuary and we also saw an oil tanker explode and watched it burn for three or four days. However, the office didn't feel best placed when Shoebury was bombed and most of the bombs seemed to fall on the foreshore. From our window we once saw fifty enemy bombers flying right overhead towards Rochford.

Peter Brewer

FUN IN THE AIR RAID SHELTER

There was a large isle in the mud about a quarter of a mile off shore, where a bomb fell one night. How well I remember it falling – I think nearly all the windows in the village were blown out! I remember our big, plate-glass shop window was shattered. I don't think I ever realised the seriousness of the situation and it seemed quite fun to sleep in my Granny's air raid shelter in Wakering Avenue or to rush into our Morrison shelter in the kitchen when the siren went. I cannot remember being afraid.

Gloria Burwell (née Everett)

COMING HOME

When I came home for the weekend during the war and got off the train at Shoebury station the police stopped me. I told them I was going home but, of course, my ID card had my address in Waltham Abbey on it. Then they wanted to know exactly what time I would be leaving Shoebury. On the Sunday night they called at my home to make sure I'd gone.

Early in the war I was very taken with the uniform of the Land Army and volunteered immediately. Later, I found myself working on the plots opposite Bridge Cottages at Shoebury. I well remember pulling the rhubarb and digging the potatoes there in the ice.

Once, I was working at Wakering nurseries where they had greenhouses full of tomatoes when a Doodlebug came over. The foreman shouted 'Dive!' and we all jumped into the ditch with our bottoms in the air!

Eileen Whalley (née Scott)

ABSOLUTELY TERRIFYING

In early 1939 there were rumours of the possibility of war but Mr Pountney told us one morning assembly that we were not to believe these war rumours. How wrong he was!

Three doors from our house in Pentland Avenue was an electricity sub-station which was a convenient place to install the air raid siren. The first time this was activated I was playing in the garden. The noise, apart from being deafening, was absolutely terrifying and, being the first time I had heard it, I was so scared that I dashed up the garden and back into the house faster than I had ever run before!

One development that took place during 1940 was the erection of tank traps along the whole length of the seafront, in the form of large concrete blocks about 4ft square and 5ft high with just a small space between each one. Also, Shoebury Common had defences built behind the beach huts which consisted of a framework of scaffold poles which was intended to prevent access by tanks, much the same as the concrete blocks. The beach was strictly out of bounds since it had been laid with mines and was therefore cordoned off with barbed wire.

The Shoeburyness Signals, 23 November 1944. Thomas Mayhew, who worked as a telegraph operator, is bottom row, third from the right. (Tom Mayhew Jnr)

Although the air raids were not as frequent now, there was still a danger so we had a Morrison shelter installed in the living room: a steel framework about 8ft long and 4ft wide with a thick sheet of steel covering the top and wire mesh panels which clipped to the sides and ends. It was large enough to accommodate several people and strong enough to protect them should the building collapse. It was only about 2ft 6in high so also served as a dining table.

In the late spring of 1944 preparations were being made for the invasion of Europe by the Allied forces. A field close to the beach where I used to play with my friends began to fill up with military vehicles of all types, ranging from lorries to armoured cars, tanks and bulldozers.

On the morning of 6 June 1944, it was announced on the radio that the invasion had commenced. On hearing this, I ran down the road and across to the field to find it completely empty. Everything had gone during the night! Across the grass that separated the road from the beach had been laid a temporary roadway to get the vehicles across and enable them to board landing craft. Several beach huts had also been removed to gain access to the beach.

Ken English

PREPARING FOR D-DAY

For some time before D-Day, empty houses in Thorpedene Gardens were taken over by the Army and the road was filled with Army transport, jeeps and lorries, all painted with a large white star. Mum and Dad used to invite soldiers over to our house for the evening; some would bring their uniforms over and borrow Mum's iron and ironing board.

I slept in the small front bedroom and one morning when I woke up every lorry and soldier had gone and I had not heard a thing. Though we did not know at the time, it was D-Day. That day I went to Southend on the seafront bus; if you went on the top deck you could see the river over the top of the beach huts. That particular morning I saw a tug towing what looked like a very large drum, which must have been part of the 'Pluto' line to carry fuel from England to France for the invasion force. From the top of the bus I had also seen a Bren gun carrier with canvas sides in the sea and heading for the beach – this must have been practice for the D-Day landings.

John Prime

RETURN TO SHOEBURY

My family moved away from Shoebury for a few years during the war. As we travelled back on the train in 1944, I could hear the guns going continuously: bang! bang! bang!

I was aged about nine or ten and the grass in our garden in Thorpedene Gardens had grown to be as tall as I was. It was the same everywhere. Many of the houses were still empty and we used to run around and play in everyone's garden. There were soldiers in the house next door to us; they had used the banisters for firewood!

Joyce Taylor (née Robinson)

THE WAR WAS OVER

We didn't have heating in our house, just the living room fire. And we only had one lightbulb; that was in the living room where we had the blackouts put up. If we had lightbulbs in the other rooms we would have had to put up blackouts there as well.

We had an air raid shelter at the bottom of our garden and we used to sleep down there during air raids. There was us nine children, my mum and my gran. Dad didn't go in it with us. I think he thought he had to stay outside and protect us.

The first I knew that the war was over was when our neighbour, Mrs Stone, said to me 'Tell your mum the war's over.' Mum was halfway through cleaning the living room; she cleaned it every day. I said, 'The war's over' and she said, 'We've got to beat them bloody Japs yet,' and just went on cleaning without even pausing. Mrs Stone used to play the organ at the Methodist Church, and she always sung out of the side of her mouth.

Bob Dack

TEN

After the War

VE NIGHT KNEES-UP

On the night before VE Day all the ships out in the estuary began sounding their sirens and hooters. My family and all our neighbours in Wakering Avenue came out to celebrate in the street. Electric lights were hung up in the trees and our piano was wheeled out and set up in the street for an impromptu knees-up. Mother brought out the blackberry wine that she'd been fermenting in the understairs cupboard and the neighbours brought out their homemade brew. Mr and Mrs Humberstone, who owned a shop on the corner of Southchurch Avenue, were there and my dad got old Mrs Humberstone in his box wheelbarrow and wheeled her up and down while she rang a handbell to wake everyone up. She was an old Londoner and I think she was a little 'the worse for wear'! When she finally got out of the wheelbarrow, Dad found that it had been half-full of horse manure!

Wakering Avenue VE Day party in St Peter's church hall, High Street, looking towards the front of the hall. They had to have the party indoors because it was raining. Ann Burtle remembers the wonderful street decorations going up when a soldier was returning home and says, 'I had to remember to alter my prayers from "Please send Daddy home safely" to "Thank you for sending Daddy home safely".' (Doreen Penlington)

Wakering Avenue VE Day party, looking towards the back of the hall. (Doreen Penlington and Margaret Hammond)

Then some people, adults and children, went across the brickfields gathering wood and rubbish and whatever they could find, and piled it up for a bonfire in the middle of our street. The 'ack-caps', being covered in tar, went up really well! It burned all night and in the morning we found it had made a huge crater in the middle of the road!

Mr Robinson stood on the garden wall and ran an auction to raise funds for a children's party. Mum and Dad organised some more fund raising and we had a party in St Peter's church hall a few days later.

After the war, East Beach had to be cleared of mines before anyone could use it. A couple of friends of mine, Ernie Oakes and Derek Deeks, were impatient and climbed over the fence onto the beach. They set off a mine and were both killed.

The beaches reopened to the public in 1947. That was a scorcher of a summer but the winter that year was ferocious!

John Askew

RETURN FROM THE FRONT

My mother was chatting in Tucker's grocers shop in West Road one day soon after the war. She commented that Mrs Tucker would be pleased to see her son Douglas, a former prisoner-of-war, soon. Mrs Tucker explained that it could take weeks before they finally allowed him to come home. Outside the shop the bus pulled up and who should get off but Douglas! Well, they closed the shop there and then and spent the rest of the day celebrating. Douglas later came to our street party in Waterloo Road and we all celebrated together.

Eileen Whalley (née Scott)

THE THORPEDENE IMPROVEMENTS ASSOCIATION

In the winter of 1945/46 conditions between the western end of Church Road and the seafront were extremely bad, in fact almost impossible to negotiate. There was no pathway and the old 'Postman's Walk' (now Leitrim Avenue) was just a sea of mud. Maplin Way, of course, did not exist and Church Road from Cranley Gardens to the line which is now Maplin Way was unmade and, in fact, nothing more ambitious than a quagmire. The people of the Thorpdene Estate requiring a bus to Southend had a tedious walk right along Church Road and down 'Cat and Dog Walk' (now Waterford Road) and took the bus from the spot which is now Shore House.

A group of residents negotiated with the Mayor of Southend, Alderman Johnson, and Thorpe Bay Estates who owned all the land west of the future Maplin Way to improve the situation.

Thorpe Bay Estates offered to supply and fix, free of charge, a high wood-and-wire fence on the fringe of this land, a condition being that the Corporation supply a path to run alongside the fence. The Corporation wrote to me saying that they would supply and deliver, free of charge, sufficient clinker and cinder for the path if I would find the labour…

Above: Waterloo Road VE Day street party, May 1945. (Doreen Biles)

Left: Pictured at the Waterloo Road VE Day street party, from left to right, are John Scott, railway worker, Douglas Tucker, RAF, Albert Woodard, Army, and -?- Brooks, RN. They are cutting a cake iced by Eileen Whalley (*née* Scott) with the words 'Thank you all'. (Doreen Biles)

Above left: Herbert Road VE Day street party, May 1945. (Joyce Taylor)

Above right: The 18ft-high Shoeburyness War Memorial erected in 1921 was paid for by public subscription. Tom Ambridge remembers, 'Shoebury's cenotaph was originally in the middle of Ness Road at the junction with Campfield, but it was moved in the 1930s with the increase of traffic.' Les Dowie says, 'Lots of boys from Hinguar Street went into the Royal Artillery; their names are now on the cenotaph.' And Alan Cundy adds, 'There used to be an outside service at the cenotaph every year when hundreds of people attended.'

On the following Sunday morning, all the male members of the 'Thorpedene Improvements Association', sound of mind and limb, assembled on site, armed with their own spades, picks, wheelbarrows, etc, and in the course of a few Sunday mornings our temporary path was complete. This path wore well and existed for some years until the making of Maplin Way and building of the bungalows and houses at the western end of Church Road.

The Association went on to become the Shoebury Residents' Association.

Henry Evans

DO NOT TOUCH

In the early 1950s, to get to Wakering from Shoebury station I would walk to Bournes Green and take the bus to the Rose Inn, Wakering. The train timetable never seemed to coincide with the Shoebury bus. Getting to Thorpe Bay station involved a walk across fields along a farm track. It was a tortuous route, with no lights and no path.

From the end of the 1950s a bus route started along the seafront and we could finally see the sea from the bus. Before that the seafront had had barricades all across the road. There was a big red display opposite Uncle Tom's Cabin to help you identify landmines, saying 'Do Not Touch'.

Peter Allen

WATER UP BLACKGATE ROAD

The night of the floods in 1953 I heard a howling noise. It was a strange wind, different from anything I had ever heard. In the morning, when we went out the tide was coming in – up Blackgate Road. Ness Road and the area that is now Gunners Park was all under water.

Ivy Atkins (née Davis)

STEWED STEAK AND TINNED PEAS

The morning after the 1953 floods we woke up to find we had no gas as the gasworks were flooded. Our Sunday dinner consisted of a tin of stewed steak and a tin of peas heated on the open fire in our living room. The troops were sent from Shoebury to help with the rescue of people of Canvey and to fill loads of sandbags to try to stop the flood.

Margaret Hammond (née Newman)

The children of Pentland Avenue ready for their Coronation street party in 1952. Margaret Hammond says, 'My eldest brother bought a television for the occasion of the Coronation and filled his house with relations wanting to see it, but my friend Jean Kemp and I spent a rainy day at our house waiting to see it at the cinema in colour.' (Vivien Pask)

Flooding on the garrison Old Ranges in 1953. (Gillian Saggers)

Above left: Members of the St Andrew's Youth Club which operated from 1946 to 1951 seen here with Revd Jenkins, Revd Sweeny and Mrs Cook, the butcher's wife (centre). Joyce Taylor (*née* Robinson) says, 'A lot of us are still in contact today and recall our happy youth club days.' (Joyce Taylor)

Above right: John Taylor in Herbert Road with his first car, a Riley 9 Monaco, which he bought for £110 in 1953. The car was first registered around 1932. Derek Palmer remembers: 'House numbering on the Thorpedene Estate was deliberately uniform, with low numbers to the east and even numbers on the south side. Herbert Road, when first built, was numbered with evens on the north side and the Council made the builder renumber the houses to conform with surrounding roads.' (John Prime)

ON TOP OF THE TELEPHONE EXCHANGE

Dad was at the New Ranges telephone exchange on the night of the 1953 floods, covering the 6 p.m. to 6 a.m. night shift. The water came right up inside the exchange. The telephone machinery was like a piano with a deck and a high back and was put out of action as soon as the water came up, so Dad couldn't contact anyone. He had to climb on top of the mechanism and lie there all night. Mother, back home, had no idea that anything was going on, of course. Dad was rescued by a rowing boat the next morning.

Tom Mayhew

QUITE A TELLING OFF

They have made the ground higher where the new office buildings are now because in 1953 the flood came down on all that area down to the cenotaph. What I remember about that day is getting told off... I woke up on the Sunday morning and it was my job to go and get wood for the fires. I looked out of our window at Hilly Marsh and shouted to my mother, 'There's water out there!' She said, 'No there isn't.' I said, 'Yes, that's water out there.'

Instead of going out and getting firewood that day, we made rafts out of oil drums and target boards, rowing through the old tanks. Unbeknown to me, my father was over on Foulness breaching the sea walls, letting the water out. We got quite a telling off when he came back home. We thought we'd had a fun day up till then.

We couldn't get to school the usual way after the flood. We went up the footpath round the back, which is where Amstrad used to be, and then through where the industrial estate is now to Elm Road, then along Elm Road to the school.

Roger Bacon

WORKING ON FOULNESS

In 1953 I was working on Foulness Island in the offices. On the Monday after the floods, we obviously couldn't go to work and so they arranged for us to temporarily move into an office in the garrison. Later, they took us to the Foulness offices in those big Army DUKWs, amphibious vehicles. We'd meet them in the village and off we'd go in the DUKWs to work; there were quite a few people working up on Foulness so there were several DUKWs to transport us.

It was dreadful at Wakering after the floods, as I found out when I went up there to help with other members of the St Andrew's youth club. We used the kitchens at Great Wakering School and my job was to make a copper full of custard (without lumps!). I remember two little girls there who had just lost their mum and dad; it was terrible.

I loved working over on Foulness but my family moved to Upminster and I went with them.

Joyce Taylor (née Robinson)

BUCKETS FOR TOILETS

On the night of the 1953 floods I got off the bus from Southend at the end of Blackgate Road and the wind was so fierce that I could hardly walk down the road to get home. By the morning, the floodwater was halfway up Blackgate Road. Our water supply came from the Ranges and so that was cut off. We had to use buckets for toilets for six weeks. In fact, our houses had been the first in Shoebury to have downstairs flushing toilets; they had been built by Polish prisoners of war.

Vivienne Odell (née Edwards)

SEA VIEW HOMES

The Sea View Homes were five huge houses: St Christopher's, Oak, Woodlands, Amethyst and Merrytrees, set in thirty to forty acres of grounds off Ulster Avenue. Each had two massive dormitories for about ten girls and ten boys, winding stairways and wide corridors. It sounds lovely, but it used to terrify me as an eight or nine-year-old creeping up in the dark to go to bed.

Left: John Church makes his way across the frozen sea off East Beach to check on his boat, 1963. David Odell remembers, 'In the winter of 1962-63 Shoebury High Street was piled high on both sides with snow where they had made a little path down the middle. It was a huge amount of snow. Out at sea the icebergs were as high as a house. I was a driver at that time and had to go out on the sands in my DUKW. I came up against a massive block of ice; I hit it head-on and got a hole in the bottom of my DUKW.' (Ray Church)

Below: John Church with his boat moored off East Beach, pictured in 1963. Ray Church recalls, 'You couldn't tell if the tide was in or out.' (Ray Church)

I remember the USAF and Round Table giving us parties and presents at Christmas, but I also remember being forced to polish thirty pairs of shoes, peeling potatoes, scrubbing the floor and making beds. The housefather was a cruel man (I still have scars on my body to prove it) and my overall feeling about Sea View is that it was a nasty, nasty place; I was very unhappy there.

Victor Davies

POLISHING THE FLOORS

I remember the parquet floor at Sea View Homes very well – many's the time I had to clean it. You had to scrub it with white soap, then polish it and then bumper it. We had to dig out an old oak-tree root once and found a Second World War grenade and were throwing it around and playing with it until the adults found out and got the bomb squad down to deal with it. The coal bunker was an old air raid shelter.

On Sundays we were allowed in the sitting room where we were paraded in front of prospective adoptive parents and after dinner we went for long walks along the seafront.

I was caned at Shoebury High School for flicking ink, six strokes across the fingers and, because I sniggered to my friends when I went back to class, I had to go back for another six. My fingers swelled up massively.

Paul Scotchford

WE'RE STILL ALIVE!

Weekends in the '60s were usually kept for one of our favourite pastimes – drinking. Charrington's IPA in the Shoebury Hotel, Shepherd Neam at the British Legion, or Watney Red Barrel in the Cambridge Hotel.

Other places we hung out were the Ace of Hearts Café, run by Jack and Ida. Here we played on the pinball machines, fed the jukebox, listening to our favourite songs, drank coffee, Coca Cola out of glass bottles and took our lives in our hands eating Ida's food – nobody ever knew what went into her shepherds pie, but we're still alive! There was another café near the Shoebury Hotel and the Caroline Café on the seafront.

Brian Kane

CAMBRIDGE HOTEL

When I was eighteen we used to go down the Cambridge on a Saturday to have a drink. There was no other pub unless you went up to the Halfway House. There was a dancehall upstairs at the Cambridge, sometimes with a live band, and it used to be packed. They all used to flock in there; it was a hive of activity.

Roger Bacon

Terry Fane, Norman Hull and Bob Millgate entertained the customers at the Cambridge Hotel with live music during the 1960s. (Terry Fane)

DANCING AT THE CAMBRIDGE

In 1962, with my group the Toleados, I started a dance at the Cambridge Hotel from 8-11 p.m. on a Thursday evening. There were five of us in the band, all local lads. The dance was very popular with soldiers and with local girls and we ran it for about six months. I remember the Cambridge as being a plain and tidy pub with dark, wood floors and large windows, and a bar area that was large enough for us to perform in.

I later performed at the Eagle Club and at the Great Wakering British Legion. In the '80s I was back in Shoebury playing at the Conservative Club with my group Moonlight Express.

Terry Fane

ESCAPED CONVICT

One night, about 1 a.m., my neighbour in Elm Road knocked on the window and said he'd seen someone suspicious creeping around. We managed to corner this man down by Bridge Garages and I kept him there while my neighbour went for the police. The police arrived and grabbed the man and flung him in the back of their car. We later found out he was one of the Kray brothers, recently escaped from jail. He had been sleeping rough in the Shoebury train carriages. I might not have been so brave if I'd known who it was!

Les Dowie

Shoeburyness Volunteer Fire Brigade 1959. From left to right, back row: Charlie Scrivener, Ted Lester, Bill Harp, Jack Askew. Front row: Gordon Atkins, Derek Monk, Arthur Offord, Gordon Parks, Freddie Burrows, Ted Haslehurst and Phil Dore. (Trevor Harp)

Other titles published by The History Press

Front-Line Thames
MICHAEL FOLEY

The Thames has been the highway into London since early times. Iron Age forts once guarded its banks and then Roman legionaries took over. Every age since has added to the defences lining the river. But the river also betrayed the site of London to enemy airships and later aircraft. Even a complete blackout of the capital could not hide the river's route from enemy pilots. Michael Foley examines all aspects of military history around the capital and along the banks of the Thames in this fascinating new book.

978 0 7509 5050 3

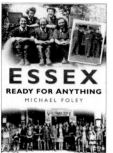

Essex: Ready for Anything
MICHAEL FOLEY

This title describes life in the county during the Second World War. It draws on written sources and interviews with people who lived through the war on the Home Front, as children or as adults. It includes subjects such as morale-boosting and fund-raising organisations, and more. Illustrated with over 100 photographs and ephemera, *Essex: Ready for Anything* will bring back memories for some, and will be an eye-opener for anyone who lives in or grew up in the county.

978 0 7509 4413 7

Southend Memories
DEE GORDON

Including many conversations with Southendians, this title aims to recall life in their town, during the 1950s and '60s. It focuses on social change, as well as school days, work and play, transport, and entertainment. It also includes memories of the late '60s clashes between Mods and Rockers, and of the infamous Wall of Death at the Kursaal. Anyone who knows Southend will be amused and entertained, surprised and moved by these stories, which capture the unique spirit of the largest town in Essex.

978 0 7509 4369 7

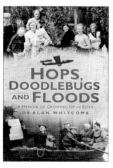

Hops, Doodlebugs and Floods
DR ALAN WHITCOMB

This is the true tale of a boy born into a typical East End family in the Second World War, beginning with his early memories of hop picking and the devastating east coast floods of 1953. The author left school at fifteen and joined the Merchant Navy, illegally, in search of a new life for £10. After a spell in an Australian prison, he returned to Essex where his fortune changed. This is an entertaining, humorous and nostalgic read for anyone who remembers Essex in the Second World War and beyond.

978 0 7524 5181 7

Visit our website and discover thousands of other History Press books.

www.thehistorypress.co.uk

An empty site within the bounds of Shoebury Garrison, photographed in 1998 and now the site of the Outlook Apartments. (Ron Henn)

PART-TIME FIREMEN

After the war, the fire service used the old air raid sirens to call the men out – they were all part-time volunteers. One hot summer's day, my brother and I were sitting on our front doorstep. They were laying storm drains in the High Street, which was causing a traffic hold-up and cars were queuing to get onto East Beach. Our dad had just taken his shirt off and sat down for his lunch when the siren went.

The people in the traffic jam looked rather worried that the air raid had gone off. What was going on? Suddenly, my dad burst out of our house and raced across the road in his singlet. Another man came running from a few doors up and another from around the corner. The holidaymakers did not know what was going on – you should have seen their faces! Me and my brother thought it was hilarious. Then the fire engine came racing out...

Trevor Harp

NOT FATHER CHRISTMAS

When I was a policeman, everyone knew me. I went into Hinguar Street School once a week and the headmistress, Mrs Sampson, picked some good kids and I'd let them have a go in the police car. I was also Father Christmas at the school, for which they gave me a bag of sandwiches and cakes. One year a little girl shouted, 'You're not Father Christmas, you're PC Cundy!'

There's a lot more people in Shoebury now, of course, living in houses where there used to be fields. Sometimes I think I preferred the cows.

Alan Cundy